think in 3D!

The 7 Characteristics Of
'Dramatically and Demonstrably Different'
Businesses

**Practical steps to improve your business
competitiveness, your competence and your culture**

Andy Hanselman and Jill White

Published by The Solopreneur Publishing Company Ltd, 9 High Farm Meadow, Badsworth, West Yorkshire WF9 1PB
www.thesolopreneur.co.uk

The Solopreneur Publishing Company Ltd focuses on the needs of each individual author client. This book has been published through their 'Solopreneur Self-Publishing (SSP)' brand that enables authors to have complete control over their finished book whilst utilising the expert advice and services usually reserved for traditionally published print, in order to produce an attractive, engaging, quality product. Please note, however, that final editorial decisions and approval rested with the author. The publisher takes no responsibility for the accuracy of the content.

ISBN 978-0-9930569-5-6

Printed in the U.K. by Charlesworth Press, Wakefield WF2 9LP

Introduction:

Hello and welcome to **3D** thinking!

This book has been written specifically for anyone starting and running a business who wants to get better at what they do.

It's based on our research and observations of some of the smartest businesses and wisest entrepreneurs. It's about what they do, how they do it, and particularly how they do it better than others.

How day after day they demonstrate that they are…

Dramatically and Demonstrably Different

Yes, that's what **3D** is all about… and it doesn't stop there. These businesses don't do it because they like the sound of it, or because they think it sounds good, they do it because it makes good financial sense. Yes **3D** businesses outperform other businesses, they achieve greater financial returns, they exceed customer expectations, and they're great places to work.

And that's why we think you should read on. We're lucky, we've met many of these people, we've interviewed them, we've visited their premises, and got inside their heads. We know you're probably too busy running your own business to do that and that's why we've written it. We've identified 7 characteristics…

The 7 'Characteristics' of 3D Businesses are:

#1: Get That Vision Thing!

#2: Think in **3D**!

#3: Create Delighted and Devoted Customers

#4: Forget CRM – Think MCR:
   '*Maximise* Customer Relationships'

#5: Create an UBER Culture

#6: KeeP In Control

#7: InnovatiON!

…and why we implore you to read this book. We want you to be **3D**.

Let's get started…

But first before you start reading this book, ask yourself this...

WHY SHOULD ANYONE BUY FROM YOU AND YOUR BUSINESS?

Before you turn the page, jot down a few things, or at least talk it through in your mind for a few seconds...

Done that? OK, now here goes...

So... did you say anything like any of these things? (Not necessarily 'word for word', but something similar)

- our 'expertise and experience'
- our people
- our location
- our reputation
- our quality
- our pricing and value for money
- our personal service
- our customer care
- our flexibility to customer needs
- our ability to solve problems
- our 'uniqueness'

Don't worry if you did as you're not alone. Lots of people do. They also often talk about their "USP's."

YOUR
USP'S... Are They

The

<u>U</u>sual

<u>S</u>tuff

<u>P</u>eople

<u>S</u>ay?

Now of course we're not saying that the things you've said are wrong, or that these aren't the reasons that customers buy from you. However, at our marketing seminars we often get people to pair up and spend a couple of minutes explaining to each other 'why someone should buy from them'. We get everyone to stand up and then sit down if they hear us say any of the words they heard from the other person. 99% of the time we have EVERYONE sat down before we've got through our short list, even if there are hundreds in the room.

We often hear people talking about their USP – that's 'marketing speak' for Unique Selling Point (or Proposition). However, we can't help thinking that in many, many cases, USP actually stands for Usual Stuff People say. Yes, most people say exactly the same thing when it comes to explaining how they differentiate themselves.

By definition, that means if EVERYONE is saying it, then it's simply not 'unique'. Of course, the things you said may well be the reasons your customers buy from you. Your challenge is to demonstrate that in everything you do.

Winning businesses **'think in 3D'** – they are **D**ramatically and **D**emonstrably **D**ifferent.

And, we want you to be the one that is different.

We want to help you to be **D**ramatically and **D**emonstrably **D**ifferent.

1. What Does 'Success' Look Like?

Before we actually share the 7 characteristics **3D** model in more detail with you let's think about 'success'. Success' means different things to different people, and therefore to different businesses. It might mean a multi-million international conglomerate that dominates world markets to some people, it might mean doing something that you're passionate about that earns you a living to others.

Whichever world you're in, the challenges facing business leaders today are greater than ever. Ever rising customer and employee expectations, increasing and intensifying competition (coming from further afield), greater transparency, reduction in trust and customer loyalty, the increasing pace and dramatic effects of change, and squeezes on resources and margins, are just some of the issues the leaders of today tell us they face.

Our experience suggests that leading a successful business, regardless of size, involves managing a balance between:

sufficient 'devoted' customers

committed motivated effective people

L

maximised financial returns

It's about;

- **Creating Sufficient 'Delighted' and 'Devoted' Customers**
- **Developing a Team Of Committed, Motivated and Effective People**
- **Maximising Financial Returns**

The 'L' is for Leadership.

Success means getting that balance in a way that works for you, your customers, your staff and your financiers. Obviously, if you're a very small business, the two base corners of the triangle mean the same people (you are likely to be the people and the financiers), whereas if you are in a large corporate business, there may well be a huge team of people, external shareholders (as well as internal customers, or 'other departments' as you might call them) all wanting different things.

The challenge is to get and maintain the balance. At one 'away day' a senior manager, of a client we were working with, came up with the great idea of creating 'delighted customers' by giving them a 40% discount. "Why don't we make them ecstatic" was our reply "… and let them have the stuff for free?" Of course it's all got to make commercial sense. Equally, it's not just about making huge profits by 'ripping off' customers or exploiting staff. It might create short term financial success, but this is all about sustainability and a long term view.

So, before we get started properly, here are 3 questions for you:

- **How does your business (or your part of your business) 'measure up' in these three areas? (Score yourself out of 10 for each area) -**
  (1) Sufficient 'Devoted' Customers
  (2) Committed Motivated Effective People
  (3) Maximising Financial Returns

- **What are the areas you need to work on? (What do you need to do to get a 10?)**

- **What do others think? (What are their scores?)**

2. What Exactly Does This 3D Thinking Look Like?

In most market sectors today, there's massive choice and an abundance of suppliers, and it's the businesses that 'stand out' that are the ones succeeding.

In this ever increasingly competitive, connected, and transparent business world, it's the 'remarkable' businesses that are thriving. **3D** Businesses are 'remarkable'? Is yours? We mean, really 'remarkable'. 'Remarkable' has to be the goal of every business. What exactly makes a business 'remarkable'? Well, in simple terms, you could say it's anything that gets people 'remarking'. Customers don't talk about 'average' stuff, 'ok' stuff, or 'not bad' stuff. They talk about 'outstanding', 'amazing', 'brilliant' and 'remarkable' stuff. They also talk about 'poor', 'terrible' 'disappointing' and 'remarkably bad' stuff. It's the businesses that create 'positive' remarks that we're focusing on in this book.

The same principles also apply to employees. We're in a world where employee expectations are also higher – finding, recruiting and keeping the people that you want is getting harder to do, and earning commitment and loyalty is a constant challenge. Add to this the ever tightening budgets, the pressure to deliver 'more for less', and the rapid pace of change, then it's no wonder that there are many stressed and overworked business leaders trying to grow and develop their business.

However, many businesses are not only surviving, but

are thriving in this ever-changing environment. How are they doing it?. What exactly makes them 'different'? How do they 'differentiate themselves and what can we learn from them?

They do things that their competitors aren't, or even better - can't, when it comes to what they offer their customers, how they lead their people and how they run their businesses. We call them **3D** Businesses and they are 'Dramatically and Demonstrably Different' from their competitors.

How do **3D** Businesses 'do it'? Well, there are no 'magical answers', but there are clearly some 'common characteristics' that differentiate 'remarkable' businesses from the rest. We've identified 7 of them which we've mentioned in the Introduction. Not a list of do's and don'ts, but some common ideas and themes on which to reflect and build a way forward for your own business and the way you lead it. And here they are again as a reminder:

The 7 'Characteristics' of 3D Businesses are:

#1: Get That Vision Thing!

#2: Think in **3D**!

#3: Create Delighted and Devoted Customers

#4: Forget CRM – Think MCR:

'*Maximise* Customer Relationships'

#5: Create an UBER Culture

#6: KeeP In Control

#7: InnovatiON!

Obviously, these 'characteristics' appear in different guises in different businesses and are very much dependent on their size, stage of growth, development, industry, and the market sectors they operate in.

Your challenge is to work out:
- **What they mean for you, your business and how you lead your business**
- **How you measure up, and crucially…**
- **Where you need to focus your resources and efforts**

We'll initially outline the characteristics in the next few pages, but then we'll go on to expand into a chapter for each one. It's up to you, how you tackle the areas… you can plunge right in and go the whole way through, or you can dip in and out of the characteristics you feel are most relevant to your business. Off you go.

Characteristic #1: Get That Vision Thing!

> *"Fixed on the vision, flexible on the journey"*
> Jeff Bezos, CEO, Amazon

3D Businesses know where they're going. All their people do too. They Establish A Clear Vision that inspires, engages and motivates everyone in the business (and often their customers too – that's what they 'buy in' to it). Not a set of financial figures or 'pie in the sky' dreams, but a meaningful picture of the future that creates focus, direction, passion and commitment. The result? Committed, motivated and effective, people at every level of the business.

Characteristic #2: **Think in 3D!**

"We go in and shake up other industries and I think, you know, we do it differently and I think that industries are not quite the same as a result of Virgin attacking the market"

Richard Branson

3D Businesses recognise that 'same as sucks' and therefore they Establish A Dramatic Difference – by doing things that make them 'stand out from the crowd'. They benefit from the power and influence of word of mouth by doing things that get customers talking about them and telling others. The interconnectedness of social media means that this is even more relevant and powerful today, and will continue to be so – that's word of mouse.

A 'Dramatic Difference' is *"an unmatchable 'bundle' of products, services, skills, methods and practices that differentiate a business from its competitors".* It's stuff that competitors aren't doing – even better, it's stuff that competitors can't do.

Characteristic #3: Create 'Delighted' And 'Devoted' Customers

"Do what you do so well that they will want to see it again and bring their friends"

Walt Disney

3D Businesses engage everyone in striving to create 'delighted' and 'devoted' customers who come back for more and tell others. 'Customer Delight' is all about *exceeding* customer expectations and 'surprising' them with the level of service they provide. It means proactively finding ways to 'go the extra mile' for their customers and 'wow' them. By definition, doing this subsequently raises customer expectations **3D** businesses relish and embrace this, and work hard to raise the bar and move **From Delighted To Devoted Customers.** They make them feel 'valued' and 'devoted' to the business; their customers subsequently have high expectations and consistently receive a great experience ('great' as defined by the customers, not the business.).

Characteristic #4: Forget CRM – Think MCR: Maximise Customer Relationships.

"Buying people's attention with a magazine or online banner ad is one thing. Earning their loyalty by teaching them forms a whole different connection. They'll trust you more. They'll respect you more"

Jason Fried and David Heinemeier Hansonn, 37 Signals

3D businesses have a passion and total customer focus throughout the business and are proactive (even obsessive) in focusing their efforts and resources to make this happen. It's not about CRM systems that too often are simply a database with lots of names in it, but it's about MCR - *Maximising* Customer Relationships. This means *'proactively developing relationships that give the best to and get the best from the customers that they want.'*

Characteristic #5: Build An UBER Culture

"We interview people for culture fit. We want people who are passionate about what Zappos is about – service. I don't care if they're passionate about shoes"

Tony Hseih, Zappos

Culture is often seen as the 'soft side' of managing a business, but often it's the hardest. In **3D** businesses, 'culture' is an integral part of the **D**ramatic Difference and creates a real competitive advantage. It's very tangible and customers experience that 'culture' simply by talking to and interacting with employees, whether it's by email, on the telephone or face to face.

Our very simple definition of 'culture' in a business is *'the way we do things around here'* and an **UBER** culture is one where everyone **U**nderstands what's expected of them when it comes to living 'the culture', the systems, and processes are all **B**uilt to reinforce and support the culture they want and need, everyone is **E**ncouraged, **E**nabled, And **E**mpowered, to display those behaviours, and are **R**ewarded and **R**ecognised for doing so.

Characteristic #6: <u>Kee**P** In</u> Control

"The solution isn't more information – it's creating meaning"

Tom Peters

In this ever increasingly fast paced world, getting and keeping in control is critical. In **3D** businesses the leaders ensure that the people who need it, get the information they need, when they need it, and in a format they understand, and that includes themselves. They establish **K**ey **P**erformance Indicators that tell them how they are doing in the areas that count. Typically it's a mixture of sales and marketing, operational performance, customer feedback, people and finance and **3D** Businesses establish their own 'recipe' of 'key drivers' and that's what they measure. They also have a clear profit focus that everyone understands.

Characteristic #7: Innovati'ON'

> *"Find great ideas, exaggerate them, and spread them like hell around the business with the speed of light"*
>
> Jan Carlzon, Former Head of Scandinavian Airlines

3D Businesses recognise that Developing their Dramatic Difference is an ongoing process, and consistently build on what they've got. They recognise that 'standing still' actually means 'going backwards' and they therefore drive and develop their Dramatic Difference continuously. It is not left to chance! It's all about 'innovation' and our definition of innovation is *'the successful exploitation of new ideas'*. **3D** Businesses have the systems, processes, and the climate to support and drive that.

So, Some Initial Things For You To Consider...

3D Thinking is a 'way of doing things'. It's a philosophy. It's an attitude. It's one that is shared at every level of the business and drives performance. It looks different in every business, and there are no simple 'lists' of things to do, or 'rules' to follow.

The challenge for every business today is to 'establish' what it's Dramatic Difference actually is, and do everything it can to Demonstrate that Difference in everything it does... and crucially, keep doing it. It's about leadership, it's about culture, it's about processes, and it's about people.

So, to finish, here are 7 Questions to get you **'3D Thinking'**

1. **Do you have that 'Vision Thing' that gives you and your people a real focus?**
2. **What's your 'Dramatic Difference' and does it really differentiate you in your markets?**
3. **Are your customers truly 'Delighted' and 'Devoted'?**
4. **Are you proactively maximising your relationships with these customers?**
5. **Does your culture create real competitive advantage?**
6. **Are you utilising information to maximise the performance in your business in the areas that count?**
7. **Is 'innovation' a way of life in your business?**

And a 'bonus' question (this is all about 'the little extras')...

- **What are you going to DO as a result?**

You might want to pause now and try out a few things; alternatively you might want to go on and study one, some, or all of the characteristics that you feel are most relevant to <u>YOU</u>.

It's your business and your book… you need to take the most appropriate step to make YOU **3D**.

P.S Remember there may be others in your business too… what do they think? Consult, engage and involve them. It's what **3D** businesses do.

3. Why 3D? What We're All Up Against

So now you know what 3D is let's look at why.

Why is this **3D** thinking so important? Why do you need to be 'Dramatically and Demonstrably Different'? There are lots of reasons. Let's look at just a few of the things that what we're up against in business today... Do any of these resonate with you?

1. We're in the 'Age of Abundance'
<u>Your</u> customers have more choice. Just 'Google' your industry sector, and see what comes up. There's abundance in almost every sector today. As businesses, we all have lots and lots of competitors, and the very nature of this 'connected world' means they are coming from far and wide.

However, it's sometimes difficult to 'stand out' because…

2. There's Lots of 'Noise'
The amount of information flying around is mind-boggling. NetBase.com highlights that there are 2 million searches on Google, 15,000 tracks downloaded on iTunes, 571 new websites created, 1.8 million 'likes' on Facebook, 278,000 tweets on Twitter, 11,000 professional searches on Linked-In, 72 hours of video uploaded to YouTube and 204 emails sent in just **60 seconds...**

It's fair to say that by the time you read this, there's even more - Yes, it's going to get 'noisier'.

It means that...

3. Customers Are Putting Up More Barriers
72% of adverts are skipped by people with PVR's like Sky+, record numbers of people have 'opted out' from receiving 'junk mail' through the Mail Preference Scheme, prevent 'cold calls' by being ex-directory, and have 'spam filters' that block unwanted emails.

It's clear that in today's noisy marketplaces, customers have to give you 'permission' to allow you to talk to them, or even approach them. They no longer just sit and wait for something interesting to come to them. They go looking for it, when they want it, and don't wait for people 'shouting' at them 'buy from us.'

4. There's Greater Transparency
Have you ever been on the website of a hotel that says; *"We offer an amazing customer experience except from on Tuesdays and Fridays when Kevin our manager is off."* Ever picked up a brochure from a bank that says *'We don't take much notice of you – unless you're overdrawn'* or the power supply mail-shot that says *"Our customers are trapped in a deal we sold them last year that they can't get out of – care to join them?"*

Of course you haven't. Every business can (and does) say wonderful things about themselves in their adverts, their webpages, their blogs and their marketing material, but it's what their customers (and past customers) say that is becoming ever more powerful. It's now so much easier to find out what they're saying – think Trip Advisor and other price comparison websites.

It means that...

5. Customer Expectations Are Rising
Want evidence?

Henley Business School says that:
- **75% of customers believe that customer service levels are the worst they have ever been and over half that statistic have complained as a result.**

Barclaycard recently revealed:
- **The average time shoppers are prepared to queue is two minutes, down from five minutes only six years ago.**

It's online too. According to PhoCusWright and Akamai:
- **57% of customers will wait 3 seconds or less for a website to load before abandoning it.**

So, the message is clear - you're in a world of increasing customer expectations and as a result...

6. Promiscuity Is Rife
Customers are 'hopping' between suppliers much more. Loyalty is becoming harder to win. Customers can, and do abandon businesses at any time for an alternative.

They might not even have done anything wrong. Customer loyalty expert Fredrick Reicheld's research indicates *"87% of defectors express satisfaction with their previous supplier"*. In other words "yes, you were ok, but I fancied a change" or "you didn't do anything wrong, but this just seemed better."

7. Customers Want What They Want, How They Want It and When They Want It

In today's 24 hour world you can listen to music when and where you want on your iPods, you can watch movies you've downloaded onto your iPad wherever you are, you can watch TV programmes again on BBC iPlayer any time, any place, you can read all the books you've downloaded onto your Kindle, (you may even be reading this one on a Kindle.) These are just some of the things in our day to day lives that we now take for granted – and so do your customers.

Accessibility to what they want, where they want and when they want it. They also want it 'NOW'.

8. They Don't Believe The Hype

In days gone by, television was the main medium, and TV adverts influenced, even shaped, our world. It was simply a case of the more loudly and frequently advertisers shouted the more effective they were. The bigger the budget, the greater the success.

Not anymore. Research indicates that many of us no longer believe the hype, and are less trusting of institutions (politicians, banks, anyone?). In other words we're a bit more sceptical. 76% of people don't believe companies tell the truth in advertisements.

The result? ...

9. Word Of Mouth (and Word Of Mouse) Influence Is Increasing

Personal recommendations have always been a key influencer in buying decisions – how much of your new business comes from referrals and recommendations? (If it's very few, then you definitely need to keep reading this book). Now it's getting easier and easier to do it, which can be good news, and bad news.

NOP World say that…
- **93% of people claim that 'word of mouth' is one of the most reliable sources of information (up from 50% in 1977), and texts, mobile phones, email, websites and 'social media' are making this easier.**

And Social Fresh research shows that:
- **92% of customers trust recommendations from people they know**
- **70% trust consumer opinions posted online.**

It's worth pointing out that 'word of mouth' only works if there's something worth talking about. People only 'remark' about **'remarkable'** stuff. Good or bad (Hint: We're suggesting 'good' stuff is the goal.)

The next trend?

10. Who Knows?

The world is moving so fast, that there are without doubt other 'trends' that affect your customers, what they think, and what they do. By definition, they affect you and your business – they provide opportunity or threat.

Your challenge is to identify 'what' and then take the appropriate actions. One thing we do know is…

"We're in the age of the never satisfied customer"

Regis McKenna

It means you've got to…

Do great things that:
- Make your business stand out from the crowd
- Build trust and confidence in your business
- Get people ranting and raving about you (positively of course)
- Ensure you keep getting better at these great things

That's **3D thinking.**

And now let's remind you again of the 7 characteristics:

The 7 'Characteristics' of 3D Businesses are:

#1: Get That Vision Thing!

#2: Think in **3D**!

#3: Create Delighted and Devoted Customers

#4: Forget CRM – Think MCR:
      '*Maximise* Customer Relationships'

#5: Create an UBER Culture

#6: KeeP In Control

#7: InnovatiON!

3 More Questions for you...

- **What do these things mean for your business?**
- **Are they opportunity or threat?**
- **How can you find out?**

OK…let's examine each of the characteristics in a bit more detail

4. 3D Characteristic # 1: Get That Vision Thing!

The 7 'Characteristics' of 3D Businesses are:

#1: Get That Vision Thing!

#2: Think in **3D**!

#3: Create Delighted and Devoted Customers

#4: Forget CRM – Think MCR:
'*Maximise* Customer Relationships'

#5: Create an UBER Culture

#6: KeeP In Control

#7: InnovatiON!

This chapter will look at how you

#Get That Vision Thing!

"If you are working on something exciting that you really care about, you don't have to be pushed. The vision pulls you"

Steve Jobs

When It Comes To Get That Vision Thing Here Are The 10 Things We See 3D Businesses Doing.

They...

1. Create it...
They establish a clear vision of the future for their business that stimulates, excites and inspires everyone in the business.

2. Establish Consensus...
There is clear agreement of that picture of the future at a senior level.

3. Get 'Buy - In'...
Everyone in their business has bought into that future picture and feels part of it.

4. Make It Tangible...
They turn their vision into clear tangible goals and targets that drive both individual and business performance.

5. Get 'Alignment'...
They ensure everyone in the business has clear objectives and performance targets linked to that vision – they all pull in the same direction.

6. Use it...
They ensure that their vision shapes and drives their day to day decisions at every level of the business.

7. Celebrate Success...
They proactively highlight and share their successes and the individuals that contribute to it.

8. Keep It 'Alive'...
They proactively keep all their people updated on progress and plans in a timely, meaningful and relevant way.

9. Work 'ON' it...
They consistently create time to think and work 'strategically' 'on' the business to review progress and look forwards.

10. Revisit And Redo It...
They consciously create time to keep looking ahead and create their next vision.

This chapter gives you some examples of 'how' they do it.

Do You Have 'That Vision Thing'?

Where will your business be in 5 years' time? What will you be doing (differently)? What won't you be doing? What will be happening that isn't happening now? What won't be happening that is? What will be in place in 3 years' time? If that needs to happen, what needs to be in place in 12 months' time? Do you have that clear picture? Do your people know it? Does it shape and focus them (and you) in your day to day activities? Lots of questions, but **3D** Businesses work hard on creating (and sharing) the answers to those questions.

3D Businesses have a clear picture of the future that 'stimulates, excites, and inspires everyone' in the business. It's worth pointing out that Martin Luther King didn't stand on Capitol Hill in 1963 and say *"I've got a strategic business plan and a cash flow forecast"*. He created a 'dream' that changed the world. We're not saying your business has to change the world, but do you have a picture of the future that 'stimulates, excites and inspires' both you and of course, your people?

So what does a vision will like?

Well it's NOT…
- Simply a set of financial figures
- A business plan
- A 'pie in the sky idea' (although we think it should stretch you')
- The words in the MD's speech at the company annual conference

A 'vision' IS ...
- A picture of the future we want
- Something that stimulates, excites and inspires
- Agreed and committed to at a senior level
- Shared at every level of the business
- A point of strategic focus for everyone to work towards
- A driver and shaper of performance

"First, I believe that this nation should commit itself to achieving the goal, before this decade is out, of landing a man on the moon and returning him safely to the earth"
John Fitzgerald Kennedy September 12, 1961

This was a vision that galvanised a nation. They didn't have the budget, the resources or the technological know-how to do it, but they found a way and on July 21st 1969 when Neil Armstrong 'took one small step for man' (Don't worry, we're not going to keep quoting 1960's political icons, but it is a great example of 'Getting That Vision Thing' - a clear goal with a timeframe – it's all about 'destination'.)

What's your 'destination'? Of course, your business doesn't have to be "shooting for the moon", but do you have a clear picture of where you want to be.

Here's a great 'real' example...

3D Demonstrated: Webmart

Webmart is a forward thinking print services business led by Simon Biltcliffe.
The business is built on 'Capitalist Marxist Principles' which means that it focuses on making profits, but shares them with the whole team.

Back in 1996 Simon set out with the vision of *"To be the best print services agency and do as much good as possible while we are doing it"* and he has now built (entirely by self-funding) an award winning successful business with a team of 42 and a turnover of £30 million.

He works hard at keeping the vision alive by establishing shared sales and profit targets and gets 'buy in' to this vision by ensuring that all employees get a share of that profit.

Their Senior EXecutive Incentive (SEXI) scheme ensures that every employee who has been there over 2 years receives significant 'percentage of salary' bonuses based on the profitability of the business.

Simon and his team work on a 3 year plan to achieve this. They consciously create time to review and develop this plan. Simon believes it's a cyclical process and has to constantly evaluated and tweaked.

Walking around their 'preposterously yellow'

(their words, not ours) Bicester office it's clear that the vision <u>drives</u> performance – visual displays show up to date progress.

They also focus on 'celebrating successes'. The 'Wheel of Fortune' is a huge wall mounted wheel with every employee's picture on it. When they hit quarterly targets, it's spun and whoever's name rests under the needle at the top when it stops wins a 'dream come true' prize – money to spend on a specific 'wish'. These have ranged from holidays, driving lessons and having their gardens done by a professional.

"Our Capitalist Principles make us the money and our Marxist Principles mean we share it fairly" says Simon.

Getting That Vision Thing - Why Bother?

3D Business Leaders like Simon Biltcliffe, tell us a clear vision can...

- Establish a bigger picture – it's the 'wood for the trees'.
- Focus energies, time, efforts and resources – yours and your peoples
- Help identify the right paths
- Shape priorities
- Attract commitment from others and energises people – particularly if they are involved in helping shape it
- Create purpose
- Energise people
- Create the link between where you are and where you're heading
- Establish standards and expectations at every level
- Help monitor progress
- Give reasons to celebrate success when you move towards it.

And finally... it can
- Accelerate growth.

Research by Growth Accelerator, a UK Government funded agency, supporting growing businesses found that **those that have consciously worked 'ON' their business and taken the time to plan, say it has put them, on average, 10 months ahead of where they would have been without planning.**

So now 3 questions for you…
- Do you have that vision thing?
- Are your people stimulated, excited, and inspired by it?
- Are you?

What Do People Want From Their Leaders?

5 key things...

- **The ability to convey a clear vision**
- **The ability to deal with challenges**
- **A commitment to high quality**
- **Valuing employees (and their opinions)**
- **Having the confidence of employees**

> Source: The Kenexa research institute's work trends research report, exploring leadership and managerial effectiveness

Unfortunately, many leaders aren't performing. For example, the report says that in the UK...

"Less than 50% of UK employees believe their leaders are 'performing effectively' in these 5 areas"

How do <u>you</u> measure up?

10 Common Barriers to 'Getting That Vision Thing'

These are just some of the things we see…

1. A Lack of Time
Very often business leaders tell us it's a lack of time. The reality is that it's a lack of *making* time.

2. It's not Seen As 'Real Work'

3D 'UnDemonstrated': "Get some proper work done!"

The culture of many businesses is that we have to be seen to be doing things rather than, perhaps 'thinking' about them. In his early days as a graduate trainee and a junior manager of a small team in a large construction business, Andy decided one day to do a bit of 'strategic' thinking to work out where his little team was heading. Having put the kettle on and sat himself down he got so engrossed in creating a strategic picture of the future, he didn't hear his boss come in. "What on earth are you doing" he shrieked as he sat there. Thinking he would get some praise for demonstrating real leadership potential "I'm doing some strategic thinking" Andy replied naively. His boss stared back and said "Well, you can strategically think yourself down to the job centre if you're not careful – get some 'proper work' done." The whole ethos was that to be an effective leader, you had to be 'seen to be doing stuff'.

3. The Focus Is Just 'A Set Of Numbers'
Clearly finances are important and it is vital that there are clear financial targets that drive performance. However, it needs to be more than that. 'Getting that Vision Thing' involves creating a real picture of goals and targets that include customers, people, and finances and all the things that make them happen. The only thing worse than just the numbers is 'no numbers at all' or something simple like targets being 'Last year's sales, plus 10%, plus hope.'

4.Unrealistic Assessment Of The Business and Its Capabilities
This is often because there is no real understanding of what's working and what isn't. It can be due to ignorance (or worse, arrogance), naivety, or a combination of both. The key? Get other people's views, thoughts and opinions.

3D Demonstrated: "Don't just listen to the HIPPOS"

That's one of, CEO at Google, Eric Schmidt's. 'Rules' when it comes to 'strategic thinking'. He believes that pay level is irrelevant when it comes to the quality of decision making and doesn't just rely on the **H**ighest **P**aid **P**erson's **O**pinion.

5. No Consensus / Agreement
The leaders and senior team want different things, and don't want to address this.

6. Collective Irresponsibility
The senior team do commit to creating a picture of the

future and feel very pleased with themselves that they agree 'we're going to do this'. Unfortunately, they don't actually clarify who is going to do it, and by when.

7. The 'Cream Sitting On The Top Of The Coffee'

This is where the vision has been created by the leader(s), but it sits there with them at the top.

3D 'UnDemonstrated' (Again.): "Guess what's in it"

When Andy was that graduate trainee, he used to understand that 'Getting That Vision Thing' was very difficult thing to do. The senior directors used to go away on 'strategic weekends' to create the company vision and they always put them up in the best possible hotels to ease the burden and pressure. They used to come back on the Monday morning with headaches and bleary eyes and it was only years later that he realised it also involved drinking lots of beer and playing pool to 6 in the morning...

It also involved filling as many flipcharts as they could and they came back laden with data and detail. They would then spend the whole week typing up and putting all the information into wonderfully detailed document with forecasts and graphs and lots and lots and lots of data. At the end of the week, they would 'brainstorm' a sexy title for it to get us all motivated. Unfortunately they never shared it with anyone – They'd walk back to their desks, put the document in the drawer and let their staff guess what was in it. Those that guessed right were the ones who got promoted.

8. Poster Posing

Lots of lovely posters on the office walls, in the reception area, on the factory floors. They look nice, and have beautifully crafted words and phrases, but they're meaningless to the people who read them, namely those who have to make it work.

9. It Doesn't Get Used

This typically means that there are no milestones or measures, no reviews, or worse, it doesn't get discussed. Often it's all of these things. Bluntly, that means…

10. A Lack Of 'Leadership'

"A leader's job is to rally people toward a better future"

'Leadership thinker' Marcus Buckingham

Work 'ON' Not 'In'...

Do you get trapped in the 'day to day' stuff? Do you get bogged down in the 'nitty gritty'? Is it stopping you and your business moving forward? Well, you're not alone.

The Working ON, Not IN report from Growth Accelerator highlights that **33% of small and medium sized business leaders say it is impossible to create time to step back** and it is seen as a bigger blockage to moving forward than the economic uncertainty they face.

In fact, **63% say they spend less than 2 hours a week leading their business and working on 'strategic' issues.** This doesn't surprise us – so many of our clients tell us that they get trapped in the day to day doing the day to day stuff. We know we do.

The challenge for many of us is to create time to 'see the wood for the trees'. It's about taking time to think and work 'strategically'.

Let us explain. There are 3 basic levels of business thinking – see if you recognise them:
Tactical: How to deal with this customer complaint or this employee idea
Operational: How to set up a system to deal with these complaints / ideas
Strategic: How to eliminate these complaints in the first place / how to generate more of the ideas that we want

'Tactical' and 'Operational' Thinking is all about working

'IN' the business and clearly it is a critical thing in making things happen 'day to day'. 'Strategic Thinking' is about working 'ON' the business and is a key characteristic of **3D** Business leaders. They proactively create sufficient time to think and work 'strategically'.

It's a key challenge for many as we all tend to get caught up in the 'day to day'. **3D** Business leaders create time to think and work 'strategically' ON their vision, ON the way forward and the 'bigger picture'. They formally diary time and work ON the key issues, challenges and opportunities, that they and their business face. Where appropriate, they proactively involve others at different levels in this process too.

3D Demonstrated: Linked-In's Jeff Weiner Blocks Out Time.

As CEO of Linked-In, Jeff Weiner regularly blocks time out in his diary just to be alone. Realising he had little time to think, he opted for what he initially thought was an 'indulgence' – he started scheduling 'nothing' in his diary.

He says these "buffers" (he creates 30 to 90 minute blocks of time without meetings), rather than kind of indulgence, were "absolutely necessary" for him to do his job.

"As the company grows larger...you will require more time than ever before to just think: Think about what the company will look like in three to five years; think about the best way to improve an already popular product or address an unmet

---

THINK IN 3D... THE 7 CHARACTERISTICS OF 'DRAMATICALLY AND DEMONSTRABLY DIFFERENT' BUSINESSES

> *customer need; think about how you can widen a competitive advantage or close a competitive gap."*

Well, why not take a leaf out of Jeff Weiner's book, and block some time in yours?

In fact, working 'ON' your business rather than 'IN' it has been shown to be one of the most impactive things leaders can do. According to the Harvard Business Review, a report by Management Research Group (MRG) suggests that a 'Strategic Approach' to leadership is, on average ten times more important than other leadership behaviours when it comes to leadership effectiveness. It was twice as important as communication, which was seen as the second most important characteristic and almost 50 times more important than the 'day to day' tactical behaviors.

Seeing The Wood For The Trees

An integral part of 'Thinking Strategically' is creating time to identify the 'Opportunities and Threats' that your business faces. Crucially, it's then all about doing something to minimise the threats and maximise those opportunities.

Research suggests that the vast majority of business leaders have the same problem. According to the Fit To Change report, over 65% of bosses believe that their businesses can't keep up with the pace of change in today's competitive markets. 57% agree that an inability to respond rapidly and effectively to change is one of the most significant risks their business faces today.

Of course, it's very, very difficult (impossible?) to predict the future, and yes, we all know that hindsight is a wonderful thing, but this extract from the HMV's first Annual Report in 2002 does, we think, say a lot…

"Contrary to some forecasts in recent years, the internet has settled down to become a worthwhile but minority channel to market. For example, internet book sales have plateaued at just over 5% of the market, and it seems unlikely that there will be sufficient demand to enable multiple operators to develop profitably."

Yes…they managed to miss the biggest single thing that impacted on their business (and many others) and the result was very, very sad.

However, they are not the only ones. Some very clever

business people throughout history have got it wrong.

For example....

"Heavier-than-air flying machines are impossible"

Lord Kelvin, mathematician, physicist, and president of the British
Royal Society, 1865

*"The telephone has too many shortcomings to be
seriously considered as a means of communication.
The device is inherently of no value to us"*

Western Union internal memo, 1876

"Who the hell wants to hear actors talk?"

H. M. Warner, Warner Brothers, 1927

*"I think there is a world market for about five
computers"*

Thomas Watson, chairman of IBM, 1943

*"There is no reason for any individual to have a
computer in their home"*

Ken Olsen, President of DEC at the
Convention Of The World Future Society, 1977

"640k ought to be enough for anybody"

Bill Gates, 1981

"By the end of the year the iPod will be dead, kaput, finished"

Lord Alan Sugar, early 2005

"Hello Dear, I'm so excited – I've just landed the absolute dream job."

David Moyes on the phone to his wife, June 2013

(Okay, we made that last one up)

So, some questions…

- **How much of your time do you spend…**
- **Thinking 'strategically'?**
- **Looking ahead and identifying the Opportunities and Threats your business faces?**
- **Working out what you're going to do as a result?**
- **Encouraging and involving others to do the same?**

Is it enough? Remember **3D** Businesses make sure they make the time, and coming up we show you how…

Simple Steps To Get 'ON'

- **Create An Appointment With Yourself**
  Go on, you know it makes sense – get your diary out, create an appointment with yourself and get thinking 'strategically'. It's all about creating a long term picture of the future for your business or part of the business.

- **Legitimise It**
  A lot of our work involves being invited in to work with business leaders to help them think and work 'strategically' and that's why many of them say that they come on our business development programmes; it 'encourages' them to take time out.

  If you work for yourself, give yourself 'permission'. If you work for someone else, get 'permission' from your boss and from your colleagues to make it happen. Thinking 'strategically' is not skiving – it's a fundamental aspect of leadership. Let them know what you're doing and why you're doing it.

- **Encourage It**
  Get others to do it too. Encourage (demand?) that your leaders and your team members create some time to think and work 'strategically'. Are your 'strategic' meetings really that 'strategic'? Do they focus on the 'bigger picture'?

Finally, 3 questions for you…

1. **Do you create sufficient time to work strategically 'ON' your business?**
2. **What do you need to do to make this happen?**
3. **When are you going to do it?**

Go on, you know it makes sense – get your diary out, create an appointment with yourself and get thinking 'strategically'.

working both tactically and

it's hard to create time

strategically is difficult

to focus on seeing the

because you get bogged down

bigger picture

in all the day to day stuff.

it's hard to create time to focus on seeing the bigger picture

What do you need to do to 'create time'?

It's what **3D** leaders do.

20 Questions To Get You Thinking 'Strategically'

Imagine it's 3 years from now...

1. Where will we actually be as a business?
2. What will we be doing differently?
3. What will actually be in place?
4. What will we have achieved when it comes to customers?
5. What will we have achieved when it comes to our people?
6. What will we have achieved when it comes to our finances?
7. What will be happening then that isn't happening now?
8. What won't be happening then that is happening now?
9. How will we be feeling?
10. What will we be most proud of?
11. What will people be saying about us?
12. What will competitors be 'envying' about us?
13. Who will our customers be?
14. What will they be getting from us?
15. How can we provide it (dramatically and demonstrably differently)?
16. What will have changed politically, economically, socially and technologically, that impacts on our business?
17. What will we have STOPPED, STARTED, CONTINUED doing in our business?
18. What will our people be doing, thinking and feeling differently?
19. What will I be doing differently?

And an odd one to get you 'thinking a bit differently';

20. Carlsberg don't run our business, but if they did what would it look like?

For each of these questions, there are some 'follow up' questions...
- Why?
- What if we don't do anything?
- What do others think?
- What are the key milestones that will tell us we're 'on track'?
- Who needs to do what... by when?

3D Demonstrated: Southwest Airlines

Southwest Airlines is one of America's most admired companies and is often highlighted as a benchmark for customer service. Even though they have been incredibly successful over the last 40 years, they don't rest on her laurels.
In January 2013, Southwest unveiled their new vision;

Our vision is to become the world's most loved, most flown, and most profitable airline.

They spelt out their goals and targets to all their employees as they recognised that to achieve this they needed every one of its employees to work together for a common goal.

They then communicated and continually reinforce their vision via 'stories'. These stories come via their Spirit magazine which highlights employees who have 'delivered', YouTube videos with real examples, weekly 'shout outs' from the Chief Executive.

This is supported by a reward and recognition programme that celebrates success.

The Questions Your People Ask...

When business leaders create a vision, these are some of the questions their people ask (the leaders, their colleagues or themselves):

- **Why are we doing this?**
- **How is this vision relevant to me?**
- **What specifically do you want me to do?**
- **How will I be measured?**
- **What consequences will I face?**
- **What tools and support are available?**
- **What's in it for me?**

The role of the leader is to help people answer these questions and 'get them engaged'.

Go On, Get Engaged

Why do people quit their job? More money? No, the majority leave because they don't have faith in their boss, feel unappreciated, and are disengaged in their work.

That's according to friends of ours, Benchmark Recruit here in Sheffield. In 2013, they surveyed over 3,000 employees who had recently switched jobs and found that…

- **22 % left their last job due to lack of faith in the leadership team**
- **19% quit because they felt "unappreciated" and…**
- **19 % left because they felt "disengaged and unmotivated"**

As Benchmark Director Louisa Harrison-Walker highlights, it's not just about the money. In fact, 'lack of financial rewards' was the fourth reason at just under 13 %.

Louisa said *"Some bosses assume that to keep staff motivated and happy you need to give them a pay rise but the survey shows this is not a priority for most employees. People simply want to feel valued, appreciated and motivated far more than having a bigger pay packet."*

3D Businesses proactively work on sharing their vision in a meaningful way and making it relevant to all their people. They also work hard at getting 'buy in'. It's all about ensuring that everyone understands where they're heading and what that 'vision' means for them.

That doesn't mean ensuring that everyone can recite the cash flow backwards, but that they have a clear understanding of where they're heading and where they fit in. There's lots of evidence that an engaged workforce is more committed, motivated and effective.

3D Demonstrated: Resolve IT

Andrew Seaton is an award-winning entrepreneur. In 2004, he founded Resolve, an IT company in Sheffield that is a leading provider of IT support, installation and network design. Resolve employs 26 members of staff and has an annual turnover of £1.2 million. He is passionate about helping people to get the most out of technology and in May 2014 he won the IoD Yorkshire Awards' "Young Director of the Year".

Andrew and his team work hard on 'Getting That Vision Thing'. They have regular 'time outs' to shape and review progress and every year, the whole team takes a day (and a night) out to work together.

"We make sure everyone knows where the company is going, and which part they play in that by taking them away once every 6 months to communicate our vision, and to discuss where the company is going" explains Andrew. It certainly seems to be working as they continue to grow and expand.

According to a report from The Temkin Group called the Employee Engagement Benchmark Study there is a strong link between the level of employee engagement and the effort and commitment of employees to that company.

They say that compared with disengaged employees, highly engaged employees are:

1. **480% more committed to helping their company succeed.**
2. **250% more likely to do something good for the company that's unexpected of them.**
3. **250% more likely to make a recommendation about an improvement.**
4. **370% more likely to recommend that a friend or relative apply for a job.**
5. **30% less likely to take a sick day.**

If 'getting engaged' is an ingredient of Getting That Vision Thing, then what does 'engagement' look like? The Temkin Group used the following 3 questions to evaluate it:

- **I understand the overall mission of my company**
- **My company asks for my feedback and acts upon my input**
- **My company provides me with the training and the tools that I need to be successful.**

In other words, people understand what's expected of them, they feel they can contribute to this and get the help and support to do so – simple stuff isn't it.
How do you and your people measure up? Why not find out by asking them?

Keeping Your Vision Alive...

3D Businesses keep it alive. It's all about maximising the potential of their people and maximising the potential of their business. They create leadership at every level and take a formal approach to setting key goals and objectives for their people and identify the key steps they need to take to achieve them. They link these to their vision and proactively review them regularly. They make it visible and tangible for their people.

3D Demonstrated: Ella's Kitchen

Paul Lindley, founder of Ella's Kitchen baby food, has a great way of engaging his team and he really keeps the vision alive for all of them in a very creative and visual way. The whole team have bought into the concept of 'Tiny Tummy Touch-points' (just how many servings of the scrumptious baby food they plan to sell). The original target when the business started out was 200 million... now as a result of expanding, introducing new products and looking at markets overseas the revised target is ONE BILLION. Wow that's some tummies (We love it.)

3D Demonstrated: Benchmark Recruit

Having heard Paul Lindley speak at a business conference co-founders of Benchmark Recruit Amy Tingle and Louisa Harrison thought they'd implement something similar in their business.

As a recruitment business they thought a great measure for them would be 'Ambitions Achieved'. This directly links to their mission of 'realising people's ambitions by giving them the job they love as much as they love their own'.

A jam jar in the office visually highlights the targets and progress so far. It's a simple but effective way to ensure everyone has the same focus in the business to reach their targets, and they can see how they've done it.

So before we move on to #Characteristic 2… Let's take a minute to reflect on #Characteristic 1:

- **Have you "Got That Vision Thing"?**

- **Have your people "Got That Vision Thing"?**

- **Does it shape and drive your business?**

"If you make your little decisions based on the big picture, at the very least you're always heading in the right direction"

Sir Richard Branson

5. 3D Characteristic # 2: Think In 3D!

The 7 'Characteristics' of 3D Businesses are:

#1: Get That Vision Thing!

#2: Think in 3D!

#3: Create Delighted and Devoted Customers

#4: Forget CRM – Think MCR:
'*Maximise* Customer Relationships'

#5: Create an UBER Culture

#6: KeeP In Control

#7: InnovatiON!

This chapter will look at how you

#Think in 3D!

"If you think you are too small to make a difference, try going to bed with a mosquito"

Anita Roddick, The Founder of Body Shop

When It Comes To Thinking in 3D. Here Are 10 Things We See 3D Businesses Doing

They...

1. Recognise That 'Same As...' Sucks...
That means doing everything they can to be significantly 'better than' their competitors in the areas that count. They are never seen as being the 'same as' their competitors.

2. Establish a 'Dramatic Difference'...
Establish a 'bundle' of unmatchable skills, methods and products/services that make their business 'Dramatically Different' from their competitors.

3. Ensure It's In The Areas That Count...
Their 'Dramatic Difference' is in the areas that customers want and are prepared to pay (more) for.

4. Demonstrate It...
They 'Demonstrate' their 'Dramatic Difference' in everything they do and their customers recognise them as 'Dramatically Different' by what they experience 'day to day'.

5. Ensure Everyone Understands...
This means that every single employee recognises what the Dramatic Difference is and the part they play in delivering it.

6. Develop It...
Their people regularly and proactively identify ways they can develop the 'Dramatic Difference' because they are encouraged to do so.

7. Stay Ahead...
They look forward, anticipate, and develop ways to improve and enhance their 'Dramatic Difference' and stay ahead of their competitors.

8. Choose 'Em Or Lose 'Em...
They have a clear understanding of the sort of customers they want to work with and focus their efforts accordingly.

9. Make Their Marketing Work...
They develop a proactive approach to finding, attracting, and keeping the customers they want.

10. Aren't Afraid To Say 'No'...
They are not afraid to say 'no' to a customer if it doesn't make commercial sense.

This next chapter gives you some examples of 'how' they do it.

What Does '3D' Look Like?

It starts with being significantly 'better' than your competitors.

Here's a grid we've developed that explains **3D** in more detail...

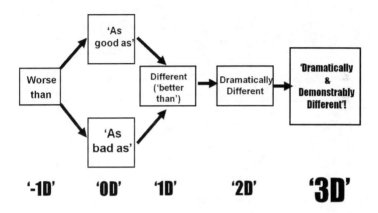

'-1D'='Worse Than': '-1D' businesses are seen as being 'worse than' their competitors in the areas that customers say count. There's a fair chance that word of mouth does impact on these business... unfortunately, it's in a negative way. People tell others to avoid them.

'0D'= 'Same As': '0D' businesses are viewed as being 'as good as' or 'as bad as' their competitors, dependent on perceptions. Whether it's 'as good as' or 'as bad as', it means what they offer is the 'same as' and 'same as' sucks. When there's no difference - they're in the world of 'complete commoditisation' and the emphasis focuses more and more on price. The only way to get better is to get cheaper.

3D 'UnDemonstrated': 'Same As' Sucks.

We once carried out a customer attitude survey for an engineering business and the results were not good. The MD was distraught as we fed back the results. He then thought about it *"How have they rated my competitors?"* He asked. "Much the same" Andy replied. *"Oh thank goodness for that"* was his response... *"Brilliant"* Andy said *"XXXX Engineering, only as crap as everyone else."* Clearly being 'as bad as' is not where you want to be.

In a bizarre way, being 'as bad as' provides greater opportunities to become competitive. The upside of it is that it's easier to create an experience that's '1D' – Being 'Different', because all they have to do is start doing some of the basic stuff right.

'1D'= 'Better Than': This means what they offer is 'Different' which is a good start. It's important that they are 'Different' in the areas that their customers say are important. There's no point being brilliant at something that customers don't value. The problem with being only slightly 'Different' is that it's often easy to copy (and overtake). Competitive advantage is like milk – it has a shelf life. What gives them an edge today probably won't do that tomorrow. The challenge therefore is to provide an experience that's 'outstanding'. They need to jump ahead, and that means...

'2D'= Dramatically 'Different': '2D' businesses often 'break the rules' or even create new ones. They may typically create a totally new experience and way of doing things which requires vision, imagination, and courage. Sometimes 'small' things can be 'Dramatically Different': for example, amazing service, great staff, speed of response, product range, the 'personal touch', technical excellence, or being 'fun' to do business with are just some of the ingredients. The challenge is to offer an experience that raises the bar of expectation, and to do this consistently.

Being 'Dramatically Different" is good – the challenge is to 'Demonstrate' that, which leads us to...

'3D'= 'Dramatically and Demonstrably Different': 3D Businesses 'Demonstrate' their 'Dramatic Difference' at every opportunity. It's a way of life. It's what they do. They are focused, they are consistent, and they are outstanding. Their reputation spreads, people talk about them, refer them, even 'champion' them, and as a result new customers come to them.

3D Demonstrated: First Direct

First Direct is the most recommended bank in the country. They're open 24 hours a day, 365 days a year. They don't have any "press 1 for..." commands - a real person answers every single call, whatever the time, day or night.

The business was set up in October 1989 and the whole ethos of it was to 'break the rules' and turn the idea of traditional banking on its head.

They've continued to do that ever since – **3D** Businesses don't 'rest on their laurels'.

They launched their PC Banking service in 1997, Text Message Banking in 1999, and Internet Banking in 2000. Now everyone has followed.

It's not just their forward thinking that sets them apart, it's the personal approach...
Jill once rang them up to speak to a specific person one morning. Unfortunately she wasn't there. Her colleague apologised and explained that she would be back later and would call Jill then. *"What time would you like her to call?"* Jill was asked. *"Oh, well I am in a meeting until about 4.30, 5 o'clockish"* she replied. *"If she called you at 5.45 would that be ok?"* came the reply. *"Yes, that would be great"* said Jill. *"Would you like us to call you at home, in your office or on your mobile?"* Jill said that the office would be good. The lady read the number out straight away, apologised again and said *'thanks for calling'*. The day went on, Jill was in and out of meetings and at 5.45 'on the button' the phone rang and a lady said *"Hello Mrs White, so sorry I wasn't here this morning – how can I help you?"*

Compare that to most banks (and businesses generally). You get a call back (maybe) when it suits them.

THAT'S what this stuff is all about – **D**emonstrating a **D**ramatic **D**ifference in day to day activities.

"an unmatchable 'bundle' of products, services, skills, methods and practices, that differentiate a business from its competitors"

Your challenge is to...

Establish Your Dramatic Difference

How can you create a Dramatic Difference? Well, basically, it's a combination of…

- **What you do...**
- **How you do it...**
- **Who you do it for...**

The best Dramatic Differences are things that your competitors aren't doing; even better, they can't do.

Here are some typical sources of Dramatic Differences.

Source 1: Be Disruptive – Create a New Model

Twenty years ago most book stores were very similar; same books, similar staff, same front windows and different logos above them. Then, in 1995 from Seattle, along came Amazon.com and the book world was blown apart, as subsequently have been many other retail industries. They totally transformed the business model and the way of doing business. Other examples include Ebay, First Direct, Airbnb, and Uber Taxis who are transforming the way you travel around major cities.

3D Demonstrated: Uber Taxis

Uber Taxis arrived in London in July 2012 with an initial team of 90 drivers. They were formed back in 2009 in San Francisco by Garrett Camp and Travis Kalanick.

The business uses its own smartphone app to connect passengers with drivers and has 'revolutionised' the way people find and use taxis.

They have completely 'broken the rules' and allow customers to go on their smartphone, enter their location and destination and up pops a price and the estimated time of arrival of a car to you. Once you press 'accept' you can track it on your phone and see it come towards you with an estimated time of arrival. Your cab arrives and off you go. At your journeys end there's no need to pay the driver – it's all 'automated' and your receipt is sent to your inbox. Simple, cost efficient and easy to use – no wonder lots of 'established' taxi drivers and firms have started protests against Uber.

The protests don't seem to be working - Uber is now in 45 countries, 100 cities and is valued at more than $15billion.

Creating a brand new way of doing things isn't something everyone can do but there are other options.

Source 2: Break The Rules

It's all about doing things your competitors aren't, or better, can't do. It's about challenging the norm and doing things different. Think Ryanair, Southwest Airlines flying cheaply with 'no frills', Metro Bank, 37 Signals, Charity: Water and the Dollar Shave Club.

3D Demonstrated: Dollar Shave Club - Razor Sharp 3D Thinking.

In a world where innovation in razors is usually yet another blade (Marketing man to MD: *'Hey, I've got a great revolutionary idea – let's add a 6th blade.'*) The Dollar Shave Club offers a Dramatically and Demonstrably Different approach.

The business was set up in 2011 by Mark Levine and Michael Dubin. Their approach is very straightforward: cheap, effective razors delivered to your door every month for a small monthly subscription. You sign up for one of three membership plans which can be upgraded or downgraded at any time. Membership fees start at only $1 a month, which they believe saves members nearly $300 a year in shaving costs.

They came to real prominence in March 2012 with their YouTube video *'Our blades are F***ing great'* which only cost $4000 to make. It's a tongue in cheek promotion of their approach and their products by CEO Michael Dubin.

At its launch the video was so popular, it crashed their server in the first hour. Once they got it back up and running, they got 12,000 orders in the first two days. The video has now been seen over 14 million times and the company has over 600,000 members, buying more that 24 million razors a year.

More products and services have been added, including shave cream and moisturizers, wet wipes and other men's toiletries. That's maximizing on the relationships with their customers (see 3D Ingredient #4 later.)

That's razor sharp thinking.

Source 3: Find The Gap

This means focussing on specific customer groups that no one else does, or can, service. The rise of the internet and today's interconnected world means that many successful businesses focus on niche customer groups and specific types of customers, wherever they may be. They recognise that they don't have to be 'all things to all people' and successfully provide very niche products and services targeted at very specific customer groups. For example, Dog TV is a TV channel for dogs – yes, honestly.

3D Demonstrated: Dog TV: Now That's Doggone Dramatically and Demonstrably Different

Dog TV was launched in the US (where else?) and is available by subscription from PTV. They launched their "round the clock" channel so that *"our beloved best friends should never feel alone again... [and] will entertain, relax and stimulate stay-at-home dog."*

So, if you have to leave your 'best friend' behind as you head out to work or go out for the evening, simply switch on DogTV and he, or she, can watch programmes specifically designed for dogs all day.

- There are shows to soothe them, stimulate them and entertain them
- The programmes are made using a technique of shooting at a level close to the ground
- They are each 3 to 6 minutes long reflecting different scenes and moods
- The colours have been changed to reflect the visual characteristics dogs respond to best
- They contain a specific soundtrack composed especially for dogs

Also, there's no advertising so your dog won't be subjected to subconscious and suggestive messages meaning that they pine endlessly for Pedigree Chum when you come home.

One million subscribers in San Diego have paid $4.99 to purchase the channel and the company has now expanded nationally across the US.

What can you learn from this approach? Well, the key thing for me is about focus. Not everyone will want to watch DogTV – cats for example – but they are not trying to reach EVERYONE.

They've clearly decided what they stand for, who they are aiming at and have focused their 'offer' accordingly.

3D Demonstrated: The iPlace is THE Place.

How do you get your restaurant to 'stand out' in the Masaxlokk area of Malta that has more than 40 restaurants all selling locally caught fish? Well a good start is *don't sell fish!*

That's just one of the **'Dramatic Differences'** of the iPlace, a restaurant that has clearly set out to be **'Dramatically and Demonstrably Different'** and judging by its Facebook page, it's certainly creating a bit of a buzz. It opened in June 2010 and for menus has over 75 iPads. As well as being able to 'see' the food you are going to order, the iPad menu automatically recommends the best wines that go with it.

You can use the iPads during your visit, and the kids can play games on them while you eat (suspect that's a bit of a win-win for parents and children alike). It clearly works as the place is apparently 'buzzing' most evenings.

Larger parties can also now get the 'celebrity for the evening' treatment as they have just launched a service that picks you up and brings you to the restaurant in their 11 foot 20 seat Hummer limousine. We suspect that works in two ways: as a very visible advert on the streets of Malta and as a 'remarkable' experience that gets people 'remarking'.

So, next time you're in Malta..... you know where to go (especially if you don't like fish).

Source 4: Solve Problems

A great way of identifying a Dramatic Difference is to spot and solve customers' problems. It could be problems they have and it could be problems they don't know they have. Did you ever crave a mobile device that plays your whole record collection whenever you want it to and wherever you are? (Think iPod.) It's often about making life easier for customers - take Mopp Cleaners.

> **3D Demonstrated: Mopp, A 3D Business That Are 'Cleaning Up'.**
>
> Mopp is a growing business that's taking a **Dramatically and Demonstrably Different** approach – they're 'making cleaning cool'. Set up by Pete Dowds and Tom Brooks in April 2013, they have adopted a 3D approach and it seems to be working.
>
> Solving 'customer problems' is often a source of **'Dramatic Difference'** and this one came from Pete and Tom experiencing that problem as customers themselves.
>
> Neither of them had any experience in the domestic cleaning business and set it up after a "terrible experience" trying to find a last-minute cleaner after a house party. After spending hours online searching for one, two no-shows and an inefficient, hungover cleaner later, the idea was born.
>
> They have grown to 11 times their original size and now have a team of 35 at their London office with

over 1,000 cleaners on board. Their **'Dramatic Difference'** is that they provide a domestic cleaning service that people can access easily online throughout London.

They clearly work hard at **'Demonstrating'** that **'Dramatic Difference'**, and use their website and social media to do this:

- **Their website is 'clean' (geddit?) and easy to use.**
- **Their blog has 'instructional' videos on things like 'how to remove red wine stains from your carpet', 'how to freshen up your kitchen' and 'how to shine up your house'. (Crowd-sourced from their cleaners).**
- **You can 'meet the cleaners – this demonstrates their 'personality' and provides the 'personal touch'.**
- **They have tips on how to get the best out of their service and your cleaner.**
- **Mopp TV, their YouTube channel, helps spread the 'word of mouse'.**
- **Their 'app' allows you to book a cleaner in 60 seconds.**

To reinforce their approach they launched this with a tongue in cheek 'rap video' which starred members of the Mopp team and this has created lots of PR via the national press and social media.

Source 5: Be Remarkable

This is all about 'remarkable' products or customer service and often both – think Apple, Ritz Carlton Hotels and Zappos.

3D Demonstrated: Zappos

Zappos.com is an online shoe and clothing shop based in Las Vegas which has 'revolutionised' clothing retailing. Set up in 1999, it has become one of the world's largest online shoe stores and is led by Tony Hsieh who set out to establish the Zappos 'Dramatic Difference' as 'creating outstanding customer experiences'. This is shaped by a culture driven by 10 core values (more of that later.)

Tony Hsieh and his executive team established 'That Vision Thing' with long-term goals for 2010: To achieve $1 billion in sales and be recognised in Fortune's list of 'The Best Companies to Work For'. In 2008, Zappos hit $1 billion in annual sales, two years earlier than expected, and the following year achieved recognition at No. 23 on 'Fortune's Top 100 Companies to Work For'.

On average, Zappos employees answer 5,000 calls a month, and 1,200 e-mails a week. They don't have scripts, and there are no limit on call times with customers. In fact, the longest call reported is 10 hours 29 minutes... (Now, THAT'S Dramatically Different.)

As part of their 'Dramatic Difference, employees are encouraged to go above and beyond traditional customer service. One 'apocryphal' story involves a late night out. Back in their hotel, Hsieh bet the guys he was with that if he called the Zappos hotline, the employee who answered would be able to locate the nearest late-night pizza place. He rang 'anonymously' and sure enough, the Zappos employee returned two minutes later with a list of the five closest late night pizza restaurants. Another example was when a woman called Zappos to return a pair of boots for her husband, because he had recently been killed in a car accident. The next day, she received a flower delivery, which the call centre rep had billed to the company without checking with her supervisor.

In 2009, the company was acquired by Amazon for a reported $1.2 billion! Part of the deal was that Amazon would let Zappos continue to operate as an independent entity with its culture and Dramatic Difference.

"We asked ourselves what we wanted this company to stand for. We didn't want to just sell shoes. I wasn't even into shoes - but I was passionate about customer service."

Tony Hsieh

OK, so you may be saying many of these businesses are multinational 'super businesses' and mine isn't. Well, we could argue that '3D Thinking' is why they are, but let's look at one last real example in more detail, in this case, a charity...

3D Demonstrated: Charity: Water – A Totally 100% 3D Approach To Fundraising.

Charity: Water was set up by Founder Scott Harrison, in 2006, to bring clean and safe drinking water to people in developing nations. Since its founding, Charity: Water has established 25 local partnerships around the world, raised over $100 million that has funded almost 8,000 projects in 20 countries, and provided roughly 1.8 million people with clean water. Their goal is to bring clean water to 100 million people by 2020.

This is what they do…

An integral part of their **'Dramatic Difference'** is the fact that **100% of the donations they raise goes direct to fund clean water projects.** Yes, 100%… They even reimburse credit card charges for those who donate online. How? They raise the money to run the charity through private donations, foundations and sponsorship. Now, THAT's **Dramatically Different.**

So, to get you 'thinking' in 3D...

- Where are the opportunities in your market to be 'disruptive'?
- What 'rules' could you break?
- How can you change the thinking from *"we've always done that"*, *"that's what everyone does"*, *"we're not allowed to do that"* to *"wow, no-one's ever thought of that!"*
- Are there any specific customer groups you're ignoring, taking for granted, have specific issues, problems and needs that aren't being addressed?
- What 'problems' do your customers have that you could solve? (Hint: they may not know they have them.)
- What 'frustrations' could you eliminate?
- What could you do to be 'remarkable'? (Focus on the things your customers 'value' and think important, not just what you're good at.)

A word of warning: Your 'Dramatic Difference' is only any good if your customers…

- # **WANT it.**

- # **RECOGNISE it.**

- # **ARE PREPARED TO PAY (MORE) FOR it.**

So, Your Challenge is to...

Choose 'Em Or Lose 'Em!

3D Businesses 'Choose 'Em or Lose 'Em'. That means they focus on the customers that they WANT to work with. They understand where their profits come from and ensure that all their sales and marketing efforts are focused on attracting and winning these customers.

They focus on specifically targeted customers and are also happy to say 'no' to those they don't want to work with. They 'position' themselves and understand that they don't have to be loved by everyone.

A report from Deloitte highlighting the UK's 1000 fastest growing medium-sized businesses, who collectively increased their sales by £45 billion in the past 4 years, shows that 60% are business-to-business organisations that operate in niche markets.

What can you learn from this approach? Well, the key thing is it's about focus. **'Choose 'Em Or Lose 'Em'** means not trying to reach EVERYONE. It means clearly deciding what you stand for, who you are aiming at and focusing your 'offer' accordingly.

3D Demonstrated: Cultivating The Customer Base

As the MD of an engineering business once told us six months after consciously cultivating his customer base, *"Having dumped my non-profitable customers, I've got more time to devote to my best customers, less hassle, increased profits, and the satisfaction of knowing my competitors have picked up all the problems that go with my old bad customers."*

Too many businesses find it impossible to say 'no', and end up taking on work that is non-profitable, proves difficult or impossible to deliver, is time consuming, and causes hassle to everyone in the business, as well as the customer. Add to this, the fact due to limited resources, this non-profitable stuff actually stops them looking for and working on the profitable work, it's easy to see how many business managers find themselves being 'busy fools'.

So, what can you do? Here's a bit of 'strategic thinking' for you...

Step One: Identify Your 'Best' Customers
First of all consider your existing customer base and identify who your 'best customers' are. These might not be the biggest, or the ones you've been serving the longest. Think about order size and profitability, levels of profitable repeat business, ease of dealing with, how price sensitive they are, whether they pay you on time, whether they pay you at all. You need to agree your own criteria that suits your business; one design business we know only works with clients they like. This actually makes commercial sense as they have to spend considerable amounts of time working with clients, and find themselves being more creative on jobs they enjoy than those they don't.

3D Demonstrated: The Milestone

The Milestone is an award-winning successful 'gastro-pub'. They achieved huge acclaim and success by starring in Gordon Ramsay's Best British

---

Restaurant TV series on Channel 4. They really put themselves, and Sheffield, 'on the map' and they're a real credit to the city.

One of the key lessons that they highlight as a key factor for success for them, was their realisation a couple of years into the growth of the business that they were trying to be 'all things to all people'. They were unfocussed, offering far too many products and had a really scattered focus. The result? Being incredibly busy, stretched to the limits, providing 'unprofitable' products (and business) and exhausted.

A decision to concentrate on things that…
1. They loved doing
2. They were great at
3. Made money…

…and created a 'milestone' moment. They have gone on to great success and of course TV stardom.

Step Two: Establish Why They Buy From You

Secondly, identify why these customers buy from you, what's important to them, what attracted them to you in the first place, how you could improve, what would they like to see you do better, and importantly, how could you do more business? Carry out a 'Customer Attitude Survey', and get a real picture of your strengths and weaknesses.

Step Three: 'Profile' Your Customer Base

Use the information gained in your sales and marketing activity. For example, 'profile' the sort of customers that you want to work with – their buying characteristics, their industry sector, size, and their needs (hint: match the profile as close to your 'best' customers identified earlier).

Step Four: Maximise Resources
Target these customers, make sure that your 'selling time', and that of your team, is spent in front of these customers – this might mean turning some potential 'customers' down.

You might consider 'incentivising' these customers to do business with you (not necessarily by discounting.), or even 'dis-incentivising' those who you don't really want to work with.

Step Five: 'Dump' Your Worst Customers
As for your 'worst' customers, consider reducing your reliance on them, and then eventually eliminating them from your portfolio. We're not advocating ringing them up tomorrow and telling them to get lost, but look at how you can turn them into profitable customers – that sometimes means saying 'no'. Your time and that of your business might be far more effective working with customers who appreciate you, and let you appreciate profits at the same time.

3D Demonstrated: Dumping In Action.

A Mongolian 'eat all you can' restaurant in Brighton banned two customers… because they ate too much. Apparently, the customers visited the Gobi restaurant twice a month for two years to take advantage of the £12 deal and the management said that they were

---

fed up with their lack of manners and the fact that they ate too much each time.

"Obviously we've paid the £12 for the buffet and it says you can have as much as you like, but apparently five bowls was over the top as far as he was concerned." said one of the 'evictees'. However, the restaurant manager said: "Basically these two guys just come in and pig out. I have put up with them for two years, but have had enough. They spoil it for everyone else and are in such a hurry to get to the food so none of the other diners can get a look in. We are not a charity. We are a business. It is our restaurant and we can tell people not to come back if we want to."

Remember, if you keep bending over backwards for those 'greedy' customers, you may well fall over.

3D Demonstrated: Nike

Even Nike get it wrong apparently. According to Fast Company, when Nike's CEO asked Apple's Steve Jobs *"Do you have any advice?"*

"Well, just one thing," said Jobs. *"Nike makes some of the best products in the world. Products that you lust after. Absolutely beautiful, stunning products. But, you also make a lot of crap. Just get rid of the crappy stuff and focus on the good stuff."*

So, some questions for your business…

1. **What does a 'great' customer look like to you?**
2. **Who are your 'great' customers?**
3. **Who are your 'worst' or 'best' customers?**
4. **Who do you want to work with?**
5. **Where should you target your efforts in winning and retaining customers?**
6. **Are your marketing efforts targeted at the right people?**
7. **Are your sales and marketing people targeting the 'right' prospects?**
8. **Are all your relationships 'profitable'.**
9. **Are your people unafraid to 'turn down' the wrong kind of work?**
10. **Is your 'marketing' working for you?**

What's your 'good stuff' and your 'crappy stuff'?

Whichever customers you choose, your challenge is to...

Demonstrate Your Dramatic Difference!

3D Demonstrated: Hans Brinker Budget Hotel: Lowering Customer Expectations Makes It Easy To Exceed Them.

Lowering your customer expectations to such levels to make it easy to exceed them is the strategy of Hans Brinker Budget Hotel in Amsterdam. Its **Dramatic Difference** is that unlike so many hotels who try and raise the bar, they lower it as far as it will go and it seems to be working.

This is what it says on their website:

"The Hans Brinker Budget Hotel has been proudly disappointing travellers for forty years. Boasting levels of comfort comparable to a minimum-security prison, the Hans Brinker also offers some plumbing and an intermittently open canteen, serving a wide range of dishes based on runny eggs."

They also 'boast' that other amenities include:
- **A basement bar with limited light and no fresh air**
- **A concrete courtyard where you can relax and enjoy whatever sunshine is available to pass the high buildings on either side on the extremely infrequent days when it's actually sunny**
- **An elevator that almost never breaks down between floors**
- **A bar serving slightly watered down beer**
- **Amusing witticisms and speculations about**

former guests' sexual preferences scrawled on most surfaces
- **The Hans Brinker Budget Hotel, Amsterdam Luxury Ambassadorial Suite (featuring the Hans Brinker's one and only bath-tub)**
- **Doors that lock.**

Daft as it sounds – it seems to work. By lowering customer expectations and doing it in a 'tongue in cheek' way they consistently meet, and clearly in some cases, **exceed their customers' expectations.** It's obviously not for everyone – they target a specific group of customers, typically student, young travellers, and people looking for a 'novel' night away. Jill for example would not be a target customer...

We're back to 'Choose 'Em Or Lose 'Em'.

More Demonstrations

Lots of businesses boast excellent customer service as a key ingredient of their '**Dramatic Difference'** – and we've seen that when it works it can be a real differentiator that creates significant competitive advantage. But how do you **'Demonstrate'** that excellent customer service to new and potential customers who have never had your 'remarkable' customer experience?

Well, obviously, your sales people will tell them, their marketing materials will reinforce it, and your customer testimonials can do it very well too. Let's be honest, no decent sales person is going to say 'we're not very good', marketing materials are bound to reinforce the positives, and most of us can find one or two customers that will say good things about us (particularly with an undisclosed 'incentive'.)

Of course, we're not saying any of these things are wrong, but the vast majority of us as customers have seen it, read it (and ignored it?) all before.

The challenge for your business is to Demonstrate it. Sometimes, it's just how you go about doing business…

3D Demonstrated: Southwest Airlines

Southwest Airlines founder Herb Kelleher clearly believes that their people are a key ingredient of their **'Dramatic Difference'** as it's the most difficult thing for a competitor to imitate. *"They can buy all the physical things. The things you can't buy are dedication, devotion, loyalty—the feeling that you are participating in a crusade,"* he said.

Southwest Airlines cabin staff are encouraged to do the announcements in a style that reinforces their own personality. Here are some of the things that their staff have been heard to say...

"There may be 50 ways to leave your lover, but there are only 4 ways out of this airplane."

"Your bags will be available on carousel x. if you do not find them, they will be available in 2-3 weeks on eBay."

"In order to enhance the appearance of your flight crew, we will be dimming the cabin lights."

Check out on YouTube some great examples of Southwest staff (including a 'rapping air steward!) 'Demonstrating their 'Dramatic Difference' (it's ok, it's research).

Sometimes, you are your Dramatic Difference...

Here are a few examples of people that are their own Dramatic Difference...

3D Demonstrated: Tim's Place: Breakfast, Lunch And Hugs

A warm friendly, personalized welcome can be a great ingredient of 'Dramatically Different'.

Tim's Place is a business that concentrates on delivering just that consistently, and their friendly welcome isn't just a smile – it's a hug!

In fact it's such an integral part of their Dramatic Difference that Tim's Place promotes itself as providing 'Breakfast, Lunch and Hugs'.

This special place is run by a special man; Tim Harris in Albuquerque. Tim has Down's Syndrome and believes that the hugs are as important as the food, if not more so. He personally greets all his guests and does all he can to make it - 'The World's Friendliest Restaurant'.

Early in his teen years, having worked in various restaurants, Tim began to dream of owning his own restaurant, and in October 2010 he opened Tim's Place. He's made 'hugs' a key ingredient of his offer and it seems to be working well. He says 'the hugs are way more important than the food – after all, food is food."

A key element of **3D** is Demonstrating that Dramatic Difference and one of the ways that Tim does it (as well as actually giving the hugs'.) is the 'Hug Counter' on the wall in the restaurant which highlights exactly how many 'hugs' customers have received.

He's another one to check out on YouTube.

3D Demonstrated… Amy's Ice Creams Ice Cream Olympics

Creating 'remarkable' customer experiences can be a key ingredient of competitive advantage.

Amy's Ice Creams is an incredibly successful chain of 15 ice cream parlours across Texas that 'wows' its customers via extraordinary tricks with, yes, you've guessed it – ice cream. How cool is that?

Amy's Ice Creams' employees do 'tricks' with the ice cream as they prepare it for you. This could include throwing ice creams scoops under their legs, behind their backs, and over their colleagues. Some stores are known for throwing ice cream across the street, where either the recipient or another employee catches it (hopefully.). Oh, and they're dog friendly.

To reinforce their Dramatic Difference, they hold their annual 'cream slingin', high flying, ice cream tossing, spade juggling extravaganza – the Ice Cream Trick Olympics. 'Expert' ice cream servers performing tricks with scoops of ice cream, and a huge crowd is always greatly anticipated to cheer them on. Events include; Decathlon, where employees do ten different tricks as fast as they can, Best Team Trick, where pairs of employees work together to complete a multi-level trick, and Best Solo Trick, where individual employees try to outdo each other with complicated tricks.

But it's not just 'Olympic' events that differentiate businesses, it's what they do day to day that can Demonstrates their Dramatic Difference.

This is a great example of applying **3D Thinking** to the day to day, 'mundane', even 'boring things' that you have to do, or customers have to do. So, you can Demonstrate you Difference in lots of little ways For example:

3D Demonstrated... Out of Office

A good friend of ours, John Lyle, who's an expert on branding, does a simple thing that 'Demonstrates' his personality and his 'Dramatic Difference'. He always ensures that his 'out of office' email reply is a personal, up to date message that slips you a bit of an insight into him and what he's up to. Here's an example:

Hello there.

Sorry I am out of the office, now on holiday until Tuesday 30th August, enjoying the sunshine and hilly delights of Shropshire and Wales and will have very little access to emails in the meantime. So, if you're happy to wait until I get back, then do no more, sit back, have a cup of tea, relax.

But if you want a quicker response, you may like to email XXX instead.

Or, if you need to speak to the office, then please call them on 0115 XXX XXXX

If it is a real emergency then please do call me on my mobile on 07973 XXX XXX

XXX when I get some 'coverage' I'll be in touch.

Thanks

John

So, What Does It All Mean For You?

What are the lessons for you from all this? Well, the challenge for your business is to ensure that your Dramatic Difference is Demonstrated in the day to day. Why not take a 'proactive approach' to assess how you measure up?

Here's how…
- Set some time aside and get your team together
- Clarify what your 'bundle' of products, services, skills, methods and practices that differentiates your business from your competitors (Hint: Find out what your customers say).
- Review ALL your interactions with customers and potential customers whether they be online, offline, correspondence, or face to face.
- Identify whether they reinforce your 'Dramatic Difference' or undermine it (Tip: Some things might do neither, but be hard on yourself and consider them negative).
- Build on things that reinforce it and stop doing things that undermine it.

So before we move on to Characteristic #3… let's take a minute to reflect on Characteristic #2

- **What's Your 'Dramatic Difference'?**

- **Does EVERYONE in your business understand and contribute to it?**

- **Do your customers recognise and value it?**

"If I'd followed all the rules, I'd never have gotten anywhere"

Marylin Monroe

6. 3D Characteristic #3: Create Delighted And Devoted Customers

The 7 'Characteristics' of 3D Businesses are:

#1: Get That Vision Thing!

#2: Think in **3D**!

#3: Create Delighted and Devoted Customers

#4: Forget CRM – Think MCR:
   '*Maximise* Customer Relationships'

#5: Create an UBER Culture

#6: KeeP In Control

#7: InnovatiON!

This chapter will look at how you

#Create Delighted and Devoted Customers

"Amazing the customer means providing unparalleled customer service, making sure every transaction goes quickly and smoothly. It means fulfilling customer needs, even anticipating them. More than that, it means turning customers into FANS. We want them to tell their family members, friends and business associates about the products and superior services we provide."

Vernon Hill, Founder of Metro Bank

When It Comes To Creating Delighted And Devoted Customers, Here Are The 10 Things We See 3D Businesses Doing.

They are...

1. Quick...
Their speed of response to enquiries, queries and complaints, consistently 'surprise' their customers (positively obviously).

2. 'Easy'...
That means 'easy to buy from' and 'easy to do business with' – both online and offline.

3. Exceed expectations...
They go that 'extra mile' to 'exceed' their customers' expectations and 'delight' them.

4. Do it consistently...
By exceeding their customers' expectations they raise the bar and consistently deliver against those raised expectations.

5. Deal with disappointment...
Things go wrong in all businesses (even 3D ones), and they proactively and consistently spot and deal with customer disappointment.

6. Empower their people...
Their people are encouraged and empowered to act spontaneously and take the initiative to exceed their customers' expectations.

7. Equip their people...

They ensure that their people are equipped with the attitudes, skills, tools, and authority to 'deliver' outstanding customer experiences.

8. Spot and remove 'blockages'...

They proactively review their customer 'touch-points' and eliminate 'blockages' or 'hold ups' that irritate or annoy their customer experience.

9. Champion their customer champions...

Their people are recognised and rewarded for exceeding customer expectations.

10. Embed customer thinking throughout...

Customers are an integral part of everything they do and on the agenda in all internal communications, team meetings, and discussions.

This chapter gives you some examples of 'how' they do it...

It's Starts With Being 'Easy To Deal With' - How 'Easy' Are You?

Being easy is the first step – that is what **3D** Businesses are. However, it can be easy to get it wrong...

3D 'Undemonstrated': Not Easy At All...

A number of years ago we were on the look-out for a DVD recorder. We'd done the research and set off for one of our local high street electrical retailers full of anticipation and excitement.

In we walked and there on the left was a rack of gleaming products, but the price differences were amazing. We were approached by an enthusiastic young man who greeted us very nicely with; *'How can I help you today?'* (just as it said in their customer care manual) Confused by the wide range of products on offer, and pointing to two different, but similarly looking models, Andy said *"That one's seven hundred and fifty pounds, and that one's only one hundred pounds. What's the difference between the two?"* In a flash, he replied *"Er... about six hundred and fifty pounds"* and then went on to read all the writing on the two little red cards in front of reach product.

He's what we call the **Sales Prevention Officer!** We'd like to stress it was not necessarily his fault, and he was trying his best, but that didn't help us. Perhaps he hadn't had the training, maybe the 'DVD person' was having his or her tea, he might have been new, or maybe, just maybe, he just wasn't that bothered. Whatever the cause, it was a 'leadership' problem.

Sales Prevention Officers exist in all sorts of businesses (that could include yours) and they are the people, systems and processes that stop your customers from enquiring, buying, and re-buying from you.

Research consistently highlights that customers biggest frustrations are things like 'lack of response', apathetic staff, overbearing and over bureaucratic systems and processes, not to mention waiting too long, automated phone systems, and piped music down the phone.

For example, research by Oracle in their 'Why Customer Satisfaction Is No Longer Good Enough' report, highlights that the top 5 things that reduce customer loyalty are:
- Being transferred between staff
- No response to an email
- Length of time on hold
- Being unable to reach a human
- Unknowledgeable staff

It's not always just about people…

3D 'UnDemonstrated' (Again!): Bradford or Barcelona?

We were once speaking at a conference at a hotel in Bradford, and as we hadn't been there before we went on their website to find out how to get there. A click on the 'How To Find Us' section of the website revealed a very nice 'Google Map'…of Barcelona!

> Luckily for the hotel that was hosting the conference, we didn't have a choice – WE HAD to go there. However, on arrival, having fought our way through the maze of Bradford (very different from Barcelona by the way), we were greeted by a receptionist who very kindly asked if we'd had a pleasant journey. We replied that we'd struggled to get there as their website had a map of Barcelona on it. *"Oh, a few people have told us that."* was his reply.

Yes, it's The Sales Prevention Officer again. We're sure you've experienced it. After all, have you ever left a shop because you couldn't get served, hung up because you were sick of pressing all those phone buttons, walked away because you were dealing with someone who didn't know what they were doing or selling, gone to another supplier because you've waited too long for the call back or the quote you were promised?

Does it ever happen in your business? We bet it does! It's clear that 'Being Easy To Buy From' is a basic 'must get right' for any customer focused business – even more so 'online', as it's just so easy to click again and move on. Sales Prevention Officers exist everywhere.

Poor customer service is costing UK businesses £15.3 BILLION. That's according to a report called 'The Cost of Poor Customer Service: The Economic Impact of the Customer Experience'. The survey suggests that 73% of consumers ended a relationship due to poor service and that the root causes are:
• Having to repeat information, that's 'having to repeat information' (sorry, couldn't resist)

- Feeling trapped in automated self - service
- Having to wait too long
- Interacting with staff who have no knowledge of the service history (or customer value)
- Being unable to easily switch between communication channels.

3D 'UnDemonstrated': Marks & Spencer – Be Easy To Buy From – Andy's Mum Did Tell You

The ethos of 'Being Easy To Buy From' may seem a simple one, but many businesses still don't get it. One such business is Marks & Spencer who have been shown as having a 'high effort score' in research highlighted in Marketing Week.

The **Customer Effort Score** rates businesses on how easy they are to buy from, and the report highlighted that Iceland and Morrisons had the lowest 'effort scores', whereas Marks & Spencer was rated highest.

Although 58% of consumers say that M&S stores are clean and tidy, better rated than any other supermarket,
- **Only 17% say it does not 'take any longer than necessary to get what I need' and…**
- **Only 24% that 'it is easy to find my way around the store'.**

These ratings are lower than any other supermarket in the study. Interestingly M&S rates highly when it comes to the quality of their products, 48% of customers say that their food is always fresh and

well within use-by dates, and 46% say 'I feel like I
am buying the best quality groceries/goods possible'.
However, it might be fresh, it might be high quality,
but **if you can't find it, you can't buy it and that's a
problem.**

Now if they'd listened to their customers, they would
have discovered this some time ago - Andy's mum, a
'traditional' Marks & Spencer customer for some 40
plus years has been telling us you can't find your way
around at all (and all her friends agree, apparently!).

So, what's the answer? Well, here's one approach:

3D Demonstrated... The JC Penney's Dropped!

US Retailer JC Penney have equipped each of their
staff with an iPod Touch. This allows them to help
their customers anywhere and everywhere in the
store.

*"We want to make the process of shopping at J.C.
Penney as easy and seamless as possible."* Kate
Coultas of JC Penney explained.

So yes, they're improving the customer experience,
but it doesn't end there. They are also using the
iPods to...
- **Allow staff to view training sessions**
- **Illustrate the display layouts to maintain
  quality and consistency**

and crucially even....

- **Scan purchases and check them out**

The devices have a special plastic case that incorporates a UPC code scanner and a credit card swiping device, so customers never have to go to a cash register counter. Customers can "sign" their purchases using their fingertip on the screen.

Now **THAT** is being **'easy to buy from'**.

Where Are YOUR 'Sales Prevention Officers'?

We can assure you, they do exist in your business. They exist in every business. What causes them?

Typically, it's your

Systems and Processes... *They are geared around the business needs and not the customers, "computer says 'no'!", as long as people 'follow the system' then they are ok, they just don't work.*

Some examples:
- Ringing at 4.45pm and getting an answerphone (advertised opening hours 8.00am to 6.00pm)
- *"Your call is very important to us - please hold"*
- Being passed to 4 different people when enquiring about customer care training. (A competitor of ours when a friend rang to check them out!)
- The website that has the 'latest news' 6 months old (they were a PR business!)
- Receiving a letter that says 'Dear Sir/Madam' from a personal business advisor who'd spent an afternoon with Andy (must have been the skirt he was wearing that confused him!)
- "Closed for customer service training!"

Attitudes... *People are allowed to 'not bother', 'mediocrity' is tolerated, no clear standards set or monitored, and the reward for doing it well is that you get to do more work.*

Some examples:

- *"It's not my job"*
- Not returning phone calls (often senior people)
- Car parking for senior people only nearest the reception
- Not picking up other people's phones when they're not in

Policies... *Written policies that reinforce the wrong behaviours, standard' policies in a non – standard world, 'unwritten' policies that everyone quotes to justify their behaviours.*

Some examples:
- Being charged to park in the customer car park
- Support / help / customer care lines that 'cost'. Why should it be the customer that pays if they've got a problem, question or query about something you've supplied?
- Small print
- Pp'd letters
- Discounts for new customers, but not for existing customers

'Scriptease'... *When it's easier to follow the script than interact with the customer.*

An example:
- *"Would you like any help with your packing?"* when you've got one bottle of wine at the supermarket.

There is one more cause...

It could be YOU...

Remove Your Blind Spots…

After reading this sentence you will realise that the the brain doesn't recognise a second 'the'.

Do you have 'blind spots' in your business? Yes you do. Your challenge is to identify them. How can you do this? Well, one option is to go 'undercover' just like on the TV series Undercover Boss, but for most of us it's better to do it 'up front'.

Here are some things to consider…
- **'Stand in Your Own Queues'** – find out what it's like on your 'front line' – ring up your own business, visit your own reception, depot or shop. If you're a small business and they'd recognise you, get someone else to do it for you.
- **Ask Your People** – what do they think about what's good, bad, average? A simple questionnaire can be a good start. Get someone else to oversee it, not you. Alternatively, get some pizzas in, set up a discussion group to highlight 'key issues'. (Note – get them to do it without you being there.)
- **STOP, START, CONTINUE** – find out what your people and colleagues think that your business should 'Stop, Start, Continue' doing. Again, this could be a simple questionnaire or group discussion – it's about removing the 'blind spots' we all have. Please remember; the truth sometimes hurts – you have to listen to what's said.

Whatever you do, the critical bit is **DOING SOMETHING ABOUT WHAT YOU FIND OUT!**

Having put all that time, money, resources and effort to win customers, for goodness sake, look after them.

3D 'Undemonstrated': Ring Up Your Own Business

We regularly encourage our clients and conference audiences to 'stand in their own queues'; it means 'experiencing' things as your customers do. It could be ringing up your own business, sitting in your own reception, making an enquiry, even visiting your own website.

However, you have to be prepared for what you 'experience': one participant on a programme we were running rang his business at lunchtime after we'd all agreed to do it in the morning session. He was the Managing Partner of a very well established local accountancy firm and came back looking a little concerned. *"How did it go Charles?"* Andy asked? *"I'm not really sure"* he replied. *"The receptionist answered the phone after 3 rings and said "Hello, xxxxx Accountants, how can I help you?" which I thought was excellent"* He said he then asked *"Could I speak to Charles Smedley please?"* There was a pause and she replied *"Who?"*

Turns out that the receptionist was on her lunch break and a new employee from 'accounts" had been shooed in to cover. Not her fault she didn't know he'd only been Managing Partner for 26 years and working there for more than 40.

Here's a more positive example.

3D Demonstrated: Change The Response

When Paul Meehan became Director of Customer Experience at AXA he spent a lot of time 'on the front line', and worked with his team to change the way that 'claims' were dealt with when customers called after an accident. The first thing that the 'script' required staff to ask their customers was their personal details and policy number. Paul suggested that after an accident, customers be asked *'first of all, are you ok?'*

As Paul explained, it's simple stuff, and it's about demonstrating to customers that they care. The result? The change in approach resulted in an increase in customer satisfaction levels by 40%.

Simple stuff indeed – often, simple is best.

A 'Stand In Your Own Queues' Toolkit

1: Ring up your own business...
- How is it answered?
- Is it answered?
- How quickly?
- What's your 'first impression'?

2: Ring up yourself at work...
- Is someone covering for you?
- Do they know where you are?
- Do they know who you are?
- Do they know when you'll be back?
- Is your 'out of office' message 'updated' or 'out of date'?

3: Ring up your mobile...
- Is your 'I'm not here' message 'updated'?
- Is it personalised or just 'robotic'?

4: Email yourself...
- What's your out of office email like?
- Is it 'up to date'?
- Is it 'boring, dull and standard' or is it 'personalised and relevant'?

5: Visit your website...
- Is it 'easy to use' and customer friendly?
- Is it 'up to date'?

6: Make a website enquiry...
- What's the automated response like?
- Is there one?
- How long does it take?

- How quickly does it get 'followed up'?
- Does it get 'followed up'?

7: Sit in your own reception / visit the office / shop / depot...
- Do you get a warm welcome?
- Do you get a welcome?
- How does it 'feel'?

8: Organise a 'delivery' to your home...
- Does it arrive on time?
- Does it arrive?
- What does it look like?
- What's the ongoing communication like?
- Is there any?
- Is there a 'follow up'?

9: Ring up your accounts department (Hey this is radical stuff!)...
- Are they courteous?
- Are they 'customer focused'?
- What sort of a last impression do you get?

10: Visit your Linked In / Twitter / Facebook profiles...
- Do they reflect who you are and what you do?
- Do they represent you well?
- Are they updated?
- Do you really look like that?
- What's the first impression?

11: Google yourself and your business...
- What comes up?
- Is it good, bad or ugly?
- What are people saying about you?

12: Do none of these things...
- But get someone else to do it.

If you do 'do' any of these things, then 'do' something as a result.

If the response is positive, let people know, recognise them, praise them, thank them... even reward them.

If the response is negative, find out why, work out how it can be fixed, and 'sort' it.

And that brings us to...

'Customer Delight'

When some people hear the phrase 'customer delight' for the first time at one of our seminars they grimace and with a look of despair say *'Oh no, he's been to Disneyland for his holidays – it's going to be one of those seminars.'*

So, first of all, let's state what this is not about. It is not *'Have a nice day'*, *'Missing you already'* or *'Buy One, Get 10 Free'*. Obviously, it's got to make commercial sense (hey, anyone can give stuff away). It's not a gimmick, and it's certainly not a 'one off'. In **3D** Businesses 'customer 'delight' is part of the way they do things.

So, what is 'Customer Delight'? Our definition is…

'Surprising customers with the level of service you provide'

And let's just emphasise, it's surprising them in a positive way.

It's about 'exceeding customer expectations', and the scary thing is that in many industries, that can simply mean delivering things 'on time, on budget, and in a courteous and friendly way'.

We believe that there are 6 key ingredients of 'customer delight':
*   **It creates a 'wow' reaction;**
*   **It appears spontaneous or unexpected;**
*   **It's 'personal';**

- **It makes the customer feel valued;**
- **It's genuine;**
- **And it creates a talking point. (Dramatically Different!)**

The downside of 'Delighting' your customers by 'exceeding their expectations' is that, by definition, their expectations then rise. The challenge therefore, if you're serious about this stuff, is to 'deliver' consistently to create 'Devoted' customers – customers who have high expectations and receive a 'great' experience every time they deal with you ('great' as defined by your customer that is).

Sometimes things go wrong and customers become 'Disappointed'. 3D Businesses spot and deal with 'Disappointment' swiftly and personally, to avoid 'Disaffection'. In fact in many of these businesses, the way they deal with 'Disappointment' creates more 'Devotion'.

Here's a grid that summarises the approach:

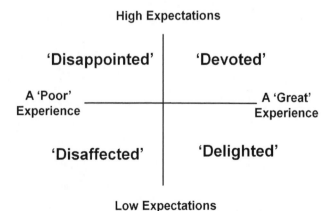

Some questions for your business
- Where are your customers currently on the grid?
- Do you have 'devoted' customers?
- Are they 'delighted'? What do you need to do to move them from delighted to devoted?
- How good are you at spotting and dealing with 'disappointed' customers?
- What can you do to transform your disaffected customers into 'devoted'?

What are you waiting for? Go do it. Go and DELIGHT them.

Because...

- **Only 2% of customers believe that customer experiences generally 'exceed' their expectations**
- **62% said they 'Meet' expectations**
- **32% 'miss' expectations**
- **(4% weren't sure.)**

American Express Global Customer Service Barometer

That is a massive opportunity!

The Benefits Of Delighted And Devoted Customers

The impact of this stuff is very tangible...

- **31% of customers purchase more from retailers after a positive experience.**

  Source: Henley Business School

- **50% of UK customers will spend more on products and services if the service experience was guaranteed to be first class.**
- **UK consumers will pay a premium of 7% for the privilege of good customer service.**
- **70% state they would do more business with an organisation that offered decent customer care.**

  Source: American Express Global Customer Service
  Barometer Report

- **In a business to business engagement, 'delighted' customers are FIVE TIMES more likely to plan on repurchasing than merely satisfied customers.**

  According to the IPSOS Loyalty Report

In other words, 'Delighted' and 'Devoted' customers...
- # Spend more
- # Come back for more
- # Stay loyal

The Ingredients Of 'Customer Delight'

So, what does customer delight actually 'look like'? Well, obviously, it's different for different types of industries, businesses and, by definition, different types of customers. What would 'delight' a corporate client of a large law firm may be very different from something that delights a teenage shopper.

So, although there are lots of ways of 'delighting' customers, what we have seen are common 'ingredients' of success. Your challenge is to work out what these 'ingredients' look like for your business, and crucially, your customers.

Your task is then to meet those needs. Even better, exceed them and create 'Customer Delight'. The reality is that 'good' isn't good enough if better was expected.

Let's look at those ingredients of 'Customer Delight'....

Ingredient #1: It Produces A 'Wow' Reaction...

3D Demonstrated: Mortons

Peter Shankman is a social media expert in the US and was flying home after a long day. Jokingly, sat on the plane before take-off, he 'tweeted'... *"Hey @ Mortons - can you meet me at Newark Airport with a porterhouse when I land in 2 hours? K, thanks)"* and switched off his phone. (For those that don't know, Mortons is a New York steakhouse). Two and a half hours later, he landed in New York and went through

to get his car, and as he walked through he heard
"Mr. Shankman – There's a surprise for you here."

Stood there was guy in a tuxedo and he was carrying
a Morton's bag. His name was Alex from Morton's
and he walked up to Peter, introduced himself, and
handed him the bag. He said that he'd heard that
Peter was hungry, and he gave him the bag. Inside
was a 24 oz. Porterhouse steak, an order of Colossal
Shrimp, some potatoes, bread, two napkins and
silverware.

Apparently they'd read his tweet, cooked him a steak,
packaged it up and delivered it some 20 odd miles
personally on his arrival at the airport.

The whole incident caused quite a stir on the internet.
They created something WORTH TALKING ABOUT.
Peter Shankman blogged and tweeted about it (he
has over 100,000 'followers'.) Others SPREAD THE
WORD too. The 'buzz' was flying all over the internet.

Now, we didn't know much about Mortons Steakhouses,
but we certainly do now, and next time we're in the US,
we're sure that they'll be on our radar.

And that's the point of 'Customer Delight' - The level
of service provided 'surprises' customers. It's not what
they expect from your industry sector and not something
they've experienced from competitors or from you in
the past. It's the returned call at the specified time, it's
the delivery that arrives early, it's the front line member
of staff who deals with your query, your enquiry, or

your problem on the spot (and doesn't have to ask a manager for permission).

Ingredient #2: It Appears Spontaneous Or Unexpected.

'Customer delight' by definition is often unexpected – the Morton's example is one where someone took the initiative (perhaps seeing a good PR opportunity?) However it's worth pointing out that some businesses build 'spontaneity' into the way they do business.

3D Demonstrated: Planned Spontaneity.

Andy once turned up at a client's office for the first time in about six months after we'd done some customer care training there. Amanda, the office junior greeted him with a smile and said *'Hi Andy, good trip from Sheffield?'* He was impressed she was expecting him and remembered where he was from. *'John will be with you in a minute, would you like a cup of coffee?' Yes please'* he replied. *'It's coffee, black, no sugar, isn't it?'* She said. *'Yes, it is...'* He said *'How did you know?' 'It's my job to know'* she replied with a smile, and went off to get his coffee. Turns out, she had a little card index system with the details of all her 'visitors' – the training obviously worked!

3D Businesses encourage and empower their people to look for opportunities to 'delight' their customers, both in a planned or a spontaneous way. It's one of the 'behaviours' that they encourage and develop in their people. In fact, in many, it's one of the things that they actually look for when they recruit them.

'Planned spontaneity' can happen anywhere in the customer journey and it's something that every (your?) business can (and should) build into its day to day activities.

'Planned spontaneity' is not a gimmick, and it's not about 'covering up' for poor products and services. It's a way of 'enhancing' the customer experience, and it's a great way of 'engaging' your people in helping demonstrate to your customers that you do actually care.

It can (and should) be built into your day to day business activities. It can help build a good framework that encourages your people to do this stuff 'on the spot' too – it's called 'empowerment'.

3D Demonstrated: KLM Surprise Team

The 'modern world' of social media provides opportunities to do this too. Willem van Hommel, was fed up because he was going to miss one of his football team's most important matches of the season, due to a trip to New York (where they don't watch much 'real' football). He 'tweeted' his disappointment on the way to the airport. When he arrived at the departure lounge and checked in, KLM Airlines surprised him with a 'Lonely Planet guide to New York' with all the best soccer bars in the city marked out for him.

The KLM Surprise Team has been set up to look at customers' social media profiles and then, using the information gained, 'surprise' them with a small 'personalised' gift when they check in such as chocolates, champagne, and traditional Dutch food. Now, THAT is 'planned spontaneity'.

Ingredient #3: It's The Personal Touch

3D Demonstrated: "Hello John, How Are You?"

Imagine calling your lawyer and when she answers the phone she says *'Hello John, how are you?"* (Obviously, if you're called John) A law firm we know have their clients' caller IDs installed and recognise their clients when they call. Clients are impressed and really appreciate the 'personal touch'. They seem particularly impressed that it happens at a law firm (maybe because their past experiences of lawyers means their 'expectations' aren't too high).

3D Businesses know and understand their customers, what's important to them and what makes them 'tick'. The key bit is letting customers know you know this. It's the unprompted bit of 'value adding information' that gets sent to them, it's the handwritten personalised ps's on letters, it's having their number on caller id (in the office as well as mobile) that allows you to recognise them when they call. It's the delivery guys who know your 'history' as a customer and your importance to the business.

> ## 3D Demonstrated: Plink Plink Fizz!
>
> We were staying for a friend's wedding at a hotel
> in North Yorkshire and as well as all the normal
> 'toiletries' in the bathroom, they'd laid on two packets
> of Alka Seltzas with a little handwritten note saying
> *'Dear Mr and Mrs Hanselman. Welcome to our hotel.*
> *We hope you have a great stay and a wonderful*
> *evening – you might need these in the morning. Best*
> *Wishes, David Stevens, The Manager'.*

We've no idea whether it was David the hotel manager
who actually wrote that note (we suspect that he didn't),
but it's a great example of the 'personal touch' that
was 'systemised' into their business. During our stay
we experienced fantastic facilities, consistently great
customer service and wonderful staff throughout. As a
result, those four tablets nicely and totally reinforced 'the
personal touch'. Result? Customer Delight!

Here's another example

> ## 3D Demonstrated: Subscribe Me.
>
> The business that decided that giving 'key' customers
> a bottle of whisky at Christmas was too 'same as'.
> The reality was that most customers simply put them
> in a 'pool' and shared them between staff – there was
> no 'relationship' or 'personalisation'. They decided
> therefore to subscribe their customers to a magazine
> for a year that they knew they'd be interested in.
> They found out their customers' personal interests

and for a similar price to a bottle of whisky provided a 'personalised' customer experience each month for a year (they had to be careful about some of their customers' personal interests!)

'Personalisation' can be a way of 'Demonstrating' Your Difference. It can come across as an 'extra', an 'addition to', and a genuine attempt to 'touch' your customers and to 'personalise' your relationships. We all like to be recognised as human beings. The 'personal touch' can be a powerful reminder to customers that someone took time out to do just that.

The reason that the 'personal touch' works so well is that it doesn't happen very often. According to a report by Pegasystems, only 4% of UK consumers feel treated as an individual when contacting their service providers including banks, telephone companies, utility providers and retailers, despite almost half of these companies claiming they offer a 'personalised' service via contact centres.

Personalised responses to customers are a great way of demonstrating you care – they make customers feel valued, and crucially, they tell others.
Obviously, by definition, 'personalisation' won't work for all customers – what works for one, won't work for another. Your challenge is to work out what this means for each of your customers.

3D Demonstrated: Chimo Holdings

The team at Chimo Holdings manufacture and export the finest quality cutlery all over the world. They've learnt how to say *'Thank you for your order'* in over 60 different languages and they then drop the appropriate hand written note inside the packaging of all their despatched goods. A quality surprise to accompany a quality product.

Ingredient #4: It Makes Customers Feel 'Valued'

As we've already seen, this can often be just a simple 'thank you'. Scarily, it could be also be something as simple as 'front line staff' taking an interest in their customers, and demonstrating that – by listening, smiling and answering their questions.

3D Demonstrated: Sainsburys...

When 3 year old Lily Robinson (sorry,3 and a half year old Lily Robinson) wrote to Sainsbury's to ask them why tiger bread isn't called giraffe bread, which she thought it should be because it looked more like a giraffe, she got a personalised response from customer manager Chris King (aged 27and a 1/3).

As well as explaining the reasons and praising Lily for her suggestion, she sent Lily a £3 Sainsbury's gift voucher.

It's simple, but effective stuff. It has a number of the ingredients of 'customer delight': spontaneous, personal, makes the customer feel valued and is 'remarkable' – people 'remark' about it.

It would have been easy to a) ignore it or b) send a standard *'thanks for your comment'* letter, but Chris's personalised response, although obviously taking a bit more effort, certainly did the trick. It also got Sainsbury's some 'free' publicity and lots of good will via 'word of mouse'.

3D Demonstrated: A Delightful Birthday Example From Yo. Sushi'... our local Yo. Sushi restaurant sent Jill a nice email on her birthday that said:

Hey Jill.

We hope we are the first to say 'Happy Birthday to you' today and unlike all of your Facebook friends, we actually did remember. To celebrate, we are giving you 1/3 off your birthday meal at YO. Sushi, but hopefully someone else is paying. Just show us your unique code at the top of this mail on your phone, laptop or old fashioned paper to claim this offer.

Many happy returns!

Team YO. Sushi

And yes, we know it's 'automated', but they didn't have to send it...and it's valid for a couple of weeks.

It's not just about sending birthday cards – how about *'Thank you – you've now been a customer of ours for 12 months / 2 years / 3 years etc.,'* or maybe a 'welcome' note after their first order. We know a conveyancing law firm that sends a *'Welcome To Your New Home'* card to its clients when they move in (and there's no bill in the card). It certainly creates a good feeling.

Ingredient #5: It's Genuine

As hopefully you've seen, creating 'delighted' customers can (and should) be systemised and built into your business processes. However, it has to come across as genuine.

The downside of this 'customer delight' stuff is that when it's done badly, it looks false and crass – from the way the phone gets answered, enquiries are handled, orders are taken, and emails are worded.

3D 'UnDemonstrated': A False Apology

A friend stayed in a holiday home in France with his family, and it wasn't good. Untidy, unprepared, run down and nasty odours were just some of the issues. On his return, he wrote a letter of complaint to the rental company. They replied promptly with a letter that apologised profusely saying that quality was a priority in everything that they did, that they'd never had comments such as this and that they were looking in to it. Attached to their letter was a photocopy of his original letter with a post it note stuck on it saying *'send usual bulls%#t sorry letter'*.

The message is clear - do not fall into the trap of 'Scriptease'- you'll get found out.

And finally...

Ingredient #6: It Creates A 'Talking Point'

The power of word of mouth (and 'word of mouse') is getting stronger. However, people only talk about brilliant stuff and poor stuff – they don't tend to talk about 'ok stuff'. The challenge therefore is to do stuff that gets people talking positively.

And now, we want to 'Delight' you... here are...

24 Ideas To "Create Delighted" Customers in Your Business

1. I saw this and thought of you... Let them know you're thinking about them by sending an email with some useful information, advice or an idea, and simply say 'I saw this and thought of you' (Do NOT send any marketing material or try to 'sell them something).

2. We were expecting you... Let your reception team know who's coming today, so they can greet people and let them know they were expected.

3. 'Get Personal'... Include ps's in your correspondence that relate to something specific about them.

4. Cards ... We don't just mean birthday cards – they can work if there's a 'relationship' there (certainly not cards at Christmas with photocopied signatures of people we don't know), but why not 'Thank you – you've now been a customer of ours for 12 months / 2 years / 3 years etc.'

5. Ask for feedback and acknowledge it specifically ... We once completed a questionnaire after staying at a hotel and mentioned a particular staff member who had been 'outstanding'. We got a lovely letter from the manager thanking us for the feedback and telling us that this member of staff was one of his 'star players' and that he'd be letting her know we'd mentioned her. Specific acknowledgement demonstrated to us that he was listening and that our opinions counted for something.

6. Give Me Space… Reserve car parking spaces for visitors and put their names on them. Preferably as near the reception door as possible. Nothing more annoying than a sign that says 'Parking reserved for Directors and senior staff only'. (Translation: 'Customer- you're not important, please clear off down the road!')

7. Ring me back… When you said you would. Give me a specific time for the call back and then do it – it's amazing how impactful that can be.

8. Ask 'How are things?'… Call me, email me and don't try and sell me something – take an interest in my thoughts and views. This works particularly well after the 'first purchase'.

9. 'Thank you for paying on time'… Do you have 'standard letters' that your accounts department send out saying 'According to our records you are 30 days, 60 days, 90 days etc. overdue'? How about a 'standard personalised' letter that says 'According to our records, you paid us on time. We really appreciate that. Thank You.' (Hey, even accounts departments can 'demonstrate' they care – this is 'revolutionary' stuff').

10. 'Is Everything OK?… The 'follow up' call after the delivery to check that everything arrived safely. Know exactly what the customer bought when you call and react proactively to whatever they say, whether it's positive or negative.

11. 'Have a Safe Trip'… A client of ours who got dropped off at the airport and was told by the taxi driver to have a safe flight, as he gave her some boiled sweets for the journey with her receipt.'

12. 'Great To See You'... The 'personalised' sign in reception with your name on it that says 'Thanks very much for visiting us today Andy – safe journey home.'

13. 'Are You Sorted?'... A call from a senior manager a few days after a complaint has been made and resolved to find out how things are now.

14. 'We'll Miss You' ... The 'sorry you're leaving us' note from the mobile telephone business who we had to leave because of the coverage problem at our new house.

15. A Phone Line Direct to you... Be accessible to customers. Even better, use caller Id to identify them when they call and greet them by name.

16. Frontline People Who Can Make a Decision 'On The Spot'... Don't allow people to say 'the manager isn't here today, can you call back?'

17. People Who 'Know Their Stuff'... People with in depth knowledge about what they are selling, understand their customers' 'challenges' and issues, 'speak their language', and give them advice that 'adds real value' and helps them make better decisions.

18. Acknowledge When You Get It Wrong... Say sorry and sort the problem quickly, and they just might stay (in fact, they probably will).

19. Support/ Help/ Customer Care Lines That Don't 'Cost'... Why should it be the customer that pays if they've got a problem, question, or query about something you supplied?

20. Give the Same Deal to Existing Customers as the New Customers You're Trying to Attract... Providing 'new;' customers with better deals suggests you don't 'value' me, or even worse, you take me for granted – that's not a good sign.

21. Even better, reward loyalty.

22. Make It Easy to 'Unsubscribe', 'Opt Out', or Say 'No'... Don't leave customers with a nasty taste in their mouth if they want 'out'. You can be sure they'll never come back if you try and 'tie them in'.

23. No Small Print... Don't try to hide things from customers – when they find out, they won't be happy and will soon become 'Disaffected'.

24. Do none of these things ... But, do 'something'. Ask your people how you can build 'planned spontaneity' into your business. There's a good chance that they'll have some great ideas that you can implement quickly and easily.

'Customer Delight' is not a gimmick, and it's not about 'covering up' for poor products and services. It's a way of 'enhancing' the customer experience, and crucially, it's a great way of 'engaging' your people in helping demonstrate to your customers that you do actually care.

So here's ours - a 'bonus' idea...

25. Ask this question...

A great way to get you started on generating ideas for Customer Delight in your business is to get your team together and complete this sentence.

If your customers were to say...

"They delivered my goods / provided their service very professionally, but what completely blew me away was..."

What do you need to do to get your customers 'blown away'?

From 'Delighted' To 'Devoted'

The downside of blowing your customers away and exceeding their expectations is that you raise them. Your challenge therefore is to deliver these things consistently to create 'devoted' customers. Customers who have high expectations and consistently get great experiences.

However, even in **3D** Businesses, things can and do go wrong. This is where they come into their own and 'Deal With Disappointment'.

Research indicates that typically 70% of people will do business with you again if you can resolve their problem or complaint, and this rises to over 90% if it's done 'on the spot'. Combine this with the fact that it costs between six and ten times more to sell to a new customer than an existing one, then this is powerful stuff.

'Dealing with Disappointment' is something that 'differentiates' **3D** Businesses from others and it can be a great source of 'customer delight'. A business that acknowledges that it got things wrong, particularly if it is 'out of character', and deals with it effectively, can often turn disappointment into 'delight'. In other words, just because things go wrong, it doesn't mean you've lost that customer. Acknowledging the problem can demonstrate that you actually care, and many will respond positively. In fact a real measure of the strength of your customer relationships is the size of 'cock up' you can make and still keep the business. (By the way, please don't take this as the key learning lesson from this chapter and test it to its limits).

The key to 'Dealing With Disappointment' is to show you care – offline and online. For example, if customers 'tweet' about your business they expect a response. And guess what, they're not getting one. The result is Customer 'Disappointment'.

A report from Maritz Research highlights the increasing expectations of customers who make a comment about a business on social media. It's a great illustration of the increasing challenges facing businesses when it comes to customer expectations. The report highlights that 51% of people who make a complaint on line expect a response, but 85% of those questioned have never received one.

Perhaps in the past (a few months ago?), you could have 'Delighted' customers by responding 'on-line' – you would have delivered a 'Great' experience that 'exceeded' their (relatively) 'Low' expectations. Not any more – their expectations have now clearly risen and responding on-line simply 'meets' expectations. Getting a response is what's expected. 'Customer Delight' is likely to come from a 'speedy response' and/or a very 'personalised' response to online comments, and with a little 'extra' something to 'wow' the customer.

3D Businesses 'empower' their people to 'Deal with Disappointment'. We're often sceptical about the word 'empowerment' because it's so over used, but in those businesses that do it properly, things get done when things go wrong. We once met a local MD who proudly told us that he'd *"empowered his people to delight their customers."* Turns out 3 years ago a couple of his team had been on a local Chamber Of Commerce Breakfast seminar on customer care for 20 minutes.

Real empowerment means giving people the training, the skills and the permission to spot and solve customer disappointment and 'delight' their customers there and then.

Here's a simple test to see how 'empowered they are. How much can they spend, or authorise, without having to come to senior management for 'permission'?

How 'empowered' are your front line people to make customers feel 'valued'?

3D Demonstrated: Timpsons

Locksmiths and shoe repairers Timpsons allow (encourage) their staff to spend up to £500 to rectify a customer's problem without management authorisation – that's 'empowerment'.

Here's an example of the 'people factor' and in particular an individual taking personal responsibility to make customers feel 'valued';

Customer Delight By Dinosaur...

When Marks & Spencer customer Bill Bennett complained that he had been overcharged for a sandwich he was told he would be sent a voucher as

---

a 'sorry' from them. It never arrived, so he complained again and asked for a cartoon of a dinosaur to be sent too to compensate for his 'inconvenience' (don't ask us why – apparently his first letter of complaint was about a £1.10 'overcharge'). Anyway, he wasn't expecting a reply.

However, Steve Jones, a customer adviser sent him a £5 gift card, and a sketch of a dinosaur with a note reading: *'Please also find a picture of a smiling dinosaur, hand drawn. Unfortunately art was never my strong point, but I hope you will appreciate it.'*

Apparently Mr. Bennett was thrilled by the response, and told lots and lots of people – it got picked up on the internet and the news spread. It's a great example of 'Dealing with Disappointment' and has some of the ingredients of 'delighting' a customer, appearing 'spontaneous', adding the 'personal touch', making the customer feel 'valued', exceeding expectations and creating a great 'talking point'.

What's even better it's about someone taking responsibility and doing something – not following a manual, a procedure or a rule. That's about 'empowerment' and 'taking initiative'. (We hope that Steve was 'rewarded' by M&S for his (art) work.)

Remember, creating great customer experiences, even when things go wrong, means that your business won't ever become 'extinct'.

So, how 'empowered' are your front line people? Are they encouraged to spot and 'Deal with Disappoint', and' to 'delight' your customers. And what 'reward' do they get if they do?

3D 'UnDemonstrated': United Breaks Guitars

A great example of failure to 'Deal with Disappointment' is United Breaks Guitars. Back in 2009 the song and video from Canadian singer Dave Carroll about his flight on United Airlines in the US, and how he got his guitar damaged by them, went viral. It started when he was told he wasn't allowed to bring the valuable guitar on board and it had to be put in the hold.

While sat on the runway awaiting take off, he and fellow passengers on board the plane saw baggage-handling crew throw his guitar on the tarmac at Chicago O'Hare airport. He raised the issue with some United Airlines employees, but they acted indifferently towards him. When he arrived at his destination in Omaha, Nebraska, he discovered that his $3,500 Taylor guitar had suffered a broken neck. Carroll filed a claim with the airline, and was informed that he was ineligible for compensation because he had failed to make the claim within the company's stipulated "standard 24-hour timeframe".

Carroll said that his fruitless negotiations with the airline for compensation lasted nine months, so then, apparently thinking what campaigner Michael Moore would have done, he wrote a song and created a music video about his experience. The song and video 'United Breaks Guitars' was posted on YouTube video on July 6 2009. It amassed 150,000 views on that first day, over half a million hits by July 9, 5 million by mid-August 2009, and over 14 million today. (You can add to this by checking out United Breaks Guitars on You Tube – it's ok, it's not skiving, it's research.)

The Times reported that within 4 days of the video being posted online, United Airline's share price fell 10%, costing shareholders about $180 million in value...

'Typically, 70% of people will do business with you again if you resolve the problem or complaint – this rises to over 90% if its' done 'on the spot'.

To conclude, here are...

5 Ideas To Help You 'Deal With Disappointment'

As we've seen, 'Dealing with Disappointment' is something that 'differentiates' 3D Businesses from others. Here are 5 things that you could do to do it too.

1. Acknowledge It. A business that acknowledges that it got things wrong, particularly if it is 'out of character', and deals with it effectively, can often turn disappointment into 'delight'. In other words, just because things go wrong, it doesn't mean you've lost that customer. Acknowledging the problem can demonstrate that you actually care, and many will respond positively.

2. 'Empower' For It. Real empowerment is giving people the training the skills and the permission to spot and solve customer disappointment there and then. Think Timpsons (OK, it doesn't have to be £500), give clear guidelines and permission for your people to 'sort it'.

3. Prepare For It. 3D Businesses accept that things sometimes go wrong – as a result, they prepare their people to spot and deal with these things. What are the things that could (and do?) typically disappoint your customers? Why not get your people together and identify typical or regular problems, and then develop ideas and solutions to sort it out. Train them, establish processes and systems to 'deal with disappointment'.

4. Look For It. Instead of just dealing with disappointment, **3D** Businesses look for it. They don't wait for complaints, they go out and find them. In fact, these businesses probably get more complaints than others because their people are actively asking for them. They also then do something about it.

So, forget 'scores out of 10' (If we get an 8 from a customer, be honest, we all subconsciously think that's ok don't we? But it's only 80%). Ask this question, if you dare: *"Are / Were you 'completely' happy?"* with the only answers being Yes or No, and then follow up with *"Why / Why not?"* Tough questions, but if you really want to know, then ask them.

As well as asking customers directly, look and listen for it too. What are people saying about you on social media? Do you know? Whose job is it to monitor that in your business? Whose job is it to then do something about it?

It might seem weird, but the easier you are to complain to, the more customer focussed you're likely to be.

5. Just Deal With It. So go on, you know it makes sense. Disappointment? Learn to look for it and deal with it.

3D Demonstrated: "Are You Completely Happy?"

This was something that was brought home to us when we got feedback from an attendee who attended a training programme we ran in a large Government department, a couple of years ago. Asked what he thought of the session, he ticked the 'Exceeded Expectations' box which looked like good news. In the next box headed *'Why?'* he wrote *'because it wasn't as rubbish as all the other training courses they've sent me on.'* That's hardly a ringing endorsement. (Marketing campaign: Hey, we're slightly less rubbish than our competitors). To be fair, when we spoke to him, he was 'completely happy'. Incidentally, somebody else once came to our seminars and ticked the box 'met my expectations'. Asked why, he wrote *'I expected it to be a waste of time, and it was.'* (We don't tend to shout about that one.)

In other words, focusing only on whether you 'met', or 'exceeded' expectations in isolation is a dangerous game – it doesn't give you a real picture – you need to know what their expectations were.

And Finally... Last Impressions Count

From an early age, we're told that 'first impressions count.' From your first day at the new school, 'freshers' week, that job interview, the induction day at work, that first sales appointment, all those network meetings. Of course 'first impressions' count, but so do 'last impressions'. The last 'interaction' with an individual, a business or an organisation is often the one we remember – provided of course that there is something worth remembering.

In other words, your challenge is to make sure that EVERY interaction your customers have with your business makes an impression, whenever possible, and make it a lasting one. As Seth Godin says *"People don't believe what you tell them. They rarely believe what you show them. They often believe what their friends tell them. They always believe what they tell themselves."*

3D Demonstrated: A Postcard From Your Dog.

Triple A, a dog kennel in the north east, sends a postcard to your home that greets you when you get in from your holidays saying *"Dear mum and dad, having a great holiday at the dog kennels, love Bonzo x x x"*. Guess what customers say when you ask if they had a good holiday *"Yes... we got a postcard from our dog!"*

So, have a think, what's the lasting impression you leave with your customers? What could you do to 'make it memorable'?

3D Demonstrated: Safe Journey Home

Andy left a hotel after a conference he'd been speaking at and as part of the 'conference team' he got a lovely personalised 'thank you' letter from the hotel manager in a little brown bag that also contained an apple, a chocolate bar, a bottle of water and a note saying *"Have a safe journey home"*

How about that for a 'nice touch'? Simple, personal, and memorable. What made the experience even better was the fact that the presentation he had been giving was all about 'customer delight'. He mentioned it in his 'follow up' notes to over 200 participants and many, many others.

So before we move on to Characteristic #4… let's take a minute to reflect on Characteristic #3

- **How easy are you to buy from and deal with? (How do you know?)**

- **What could you do to 'Delight' your customers?**

- **How could you do it consistently to create 'Devoted' customers?**

"People will forget what you said, people will forget what you did, but people will never forget how you made them feel"

Maya Angelou

7. 3D Characteristic #4:
Forget CRM, Think MCR-
<u>M</u>aximise your
<u>C</u>ustomer <u>R</u>elationships

The 7 'Characteristics' of 3D Businesses are:

#1: Get That Vision Thing!

#2: Think in **3D**!

#3: Create Delighted and Devoted Customers

#4: Forget CRM – Think MCR:
   '*Maximise* Customer Relationships'

#5: Create an UBER Culture

#6: KeeP In Control

#7: InnovatiON!

This chapter will look at how you

#Maximise Your Customer
Relationships

"The more you engage with customers the clearer things become and the easier it is to determine what you should be doing"

John Russell, President, Harley-Davidson Europe

When It Comes To Maximising Customer Relationships Here Are The 10 Things We See 3D Businesses Doing.

They...

1. Think strategically...
They develop a strategic view to creating, developing and maintaining win-win relationships with customers they want to.

2. Understand...
They understand who their 'best' customers are, what they want, and what a maximised relationships with them looks like.

3. Get Focused...
They ensure their efforts and resources are focused on the customers they want and prioritise plans to maximise those relationships and the opportunities they provide.

4. Create Dialogue, Not Diatribes...
They recognise that customers need to be engaged. As a result, they work hard at creating 'real' conversations with their customers via the appropriate channels and formats and at the frequency that those customers want.

5. Add Value...
They regularly and proactively provide customers with relevant new ideas and solutions that 'add value'.

6. Get Personal...

They make their customers feel valued by personalising their 'offer'. They know that the more 'personalised' it feels, the more difficult it is for competitors to get in there.

7. Maximise Opportunities...

As well as 'giving the best to' their customers, they also focus on 'getting the best from' them – usually in the form of repeat business, more opportunities and loyalty by ensuring that their people can spot and maximise opportunities.

8. Think 'Share of Customer'...

They identify and prioritise the customers where opportunities exist and educate them about their total capabilities. No 'heavy sells', but proactively building and maximising their relationships.

9. Listen...

They have proactive feedback mechanisms that tell them what their customers really think about them and their performance.

10. Leverage...

They recognise the power of word of mouth, and encourage (and sometimes incentivise) their customers and contacts to refer them to others.

Let's Start With MCR - What's All That About?

We meet so many business leaders who tell us they've got a real CRM focus in their business. They've invested heavily in fantastic IT systems and facilities, and have spent a lot of time and money in training and developing people. They're ready to take on the world. The reality is that all they've really got is a database with a lot of names on it, and a number of people spending a lot of time 'filling in forms'. In a world where maintaining and keeping customers is becoming an ever increasingly tough job, somehow, this approach doesn't seem to work.

We tell them to forget CRM and focus on MCR.

MCR stands for *'Maximising* Customer Relationships':

> *"Proactively developing relationships that give the best to, and get the best from, the customers you want".*

It's not about databases, it's about relationships, and it's about maximising them. Of course, we're not knocking databases, but **3D** Businesses know it's what you do with the stuff that's in them that counts.

We've put together this simple model to help you look at your relationships (Remember, this can include 'internal' customers too).

Your Objectives Achieved

'Taking Relationship'	'Maximised Relationship'
Customer's Objectives Not Achieved	Customer's Objectives Achieved
'Losing Relationship'	'Giving Relationship'

Your Objectives Not Achieved

So, how do your relationships measure up? To help you see where you are, here are some simple descriptions - clearly they are 'different' for each type of business, sector or customer, but hopefully they give you a 'feel' for what they look like. Your challenge is to work out what these relationships look like for your business, and crucially, for your customers.

'Giving Relationship': The customer is doing very well out of this relationships but you're not. Perhaps it's the customer who constantly asks 'can you just?', consistently receives discounts, or regularly plays you off against your competitors. Are you 'giving too much away', or not charging for things you could or should? A couple of key questions to consider: Is the relationship here because you've 'allowed it', or because you've been 'pushed' into it? If it's the former, what can you do to 'educate' your customer, and try to get things on a better footing for you - if they value what you do, you may be pleasantly surprised what they'll pay for. If it's the latter, which way is this relationship going? At what point are you prepared to say 'no' or 'enough's enough'? Because if you don't you could be heading for a...

'Losing Relationship': Neither of you are winning, but guess who the customer blames (and tells others about)? What can you do to get out of this type of relationship (or maybe out of the relationship itself?) 'Taking Relationship': In the short term, this looks good - it works for you... until the customer finds out. Are there more things that you could / should be doing for your customer to 'maximise' the relationship? This could also mean 'educating' the customer about your full range of products and services so that they can get the best from you (this might result in more business.) and move towards becoming a...

'Maximised Relationship': It's win - win. It could be a very simple transaction - you're easy to do business with, the customer gets what they want and they pay you (on time.). Equally, it could be an 'in-depth', trusted and ongoing relationship, maybe even a partnership or joint venture. Again, it's defined by you and crucially, your customer.

Maximised relationships are the goal and very rarely 'just happen'. They are all about understanding your customer's goals and objectives, and working hard to help them achieve them. Obviously, it's about you achieving yours too, whether that means sales and profit margins, customer loyalty, levels of repeat business, or other specified targets specific to your business. The critical bit is ensuring that you do actually know what you want to achieve, and so does everyone in your business.

So, 7 questions that you might want to consider:

1. **Do you have a clear picture of what you want from your customer relationships?**
2. **Whereabouts on this grid are your key customer relationships?**
3. **How do you actually know? (Hint: ask your customers)**
4. **What can you do to find out? (Hint: see above)**
5. **Which way are those relationships heading?**
6. **What are you doing / need to do to get them where you want them?**
7. **What do other members of your team / business think? (Hint: ask them)**

Maximising customer relationships doesn't just happen by chance... it's a proactive process and needs to involve everyone in the business. Your challenge is to work out what 'Maximised Customer Relationships' means for you and what you can do to create them. It's then about creating your own 'recipe for success'.

Knowing Me, Knowing You –
The Key To MCR

Take two customers:
**Customer 1: Male; Born 1948: Grew up in England;
Second Marriage: 2 Children: Successful; Wealthy:
Enjoys skiing in the Alps in Winter; Likes dogs**

**Customer 2: Male; Born 1948: Grew up in England;
Second Marriage: 6 Children: Successful; Wealthy:
Enjoys skiing in the Alps in Winter; Likes dogs**

You'd think there'd be similarities right? The
'demographics' say so. Well, if you have a look later*,
you'll see who these two customers actually are. We
can't help thinking that they are a little bit different.

We often hear people talking about 'segmentation' which
is a way of 'grouping' customers together and sending
the appropriate messages to these groups. Traditionally,
we were often told to use 'demographics' to do this
– people with similar 'characteristics' – age, family
circumstances, income etc., but they often ignored
things like 'interests', attitudes, values' – all important
things that influence people's needs and wants, and
therefore their buying behaviours. The example above
was highlighted by digital analyst and best-selling author
Brian Solis and it illustrates the danger of just using
'demographics'.

3D Businesses recognise that understanding their
customers and showing them they know them can be
a real differentiator. Creating personalised customer
experiences is a key ingredient of 'Dramatic Difference'

in many **3D** Businesses. The way they do this ranges from the local pub that recognises their customers when they walk in and knows their 'regular tipple' (a pint of Dark Hart at The Beehive, Harthill thanks Emma) to the sophisticated use of BIG DATA and technology which precisely tracks customers' buying patterns and habits and responds accordingly (think Amazon: *you recently purchased, you might like…*).

Whichever way you do it, in order to sell (more) to your customers, a key factor for success is getting to know them – we mean *really* know them.

*Oh, and by the way? the two 'customers' we described were….. Prince Charles and Ozzy Osborne.

What Do You Need To Know?

3D Businesses know their customers and use this information to build, develop and maximise relationships. How well do you know your customers? What's important to them? When and why do they buy from you? They also understand what their customers want and need and what makes them 'tick'.

MCR involves a proactive approach to finding out, sharing and using this information in your business so that EVERYONE can build and maximise those relationships.

So, what should you 'understand'? Well, we see **3D** Businesses get a good understanding of their customers'

- **Perception of their performance and their capabilities**
- **Needs, problems and aspirations**

And them

- **Personally**

How do you measure up?

Let's look at you and your customers. You need to understand their perception of:

Your Performance...
- Establish a clear picture of how your customers view what you do for them. This could include:
- How do they think you are doing in providing your products/services to them?
- What do you do well?

- What don't you do so well?
- How well do you satisfy/exceed their expectations?
- What could you do to improve?
- How do you compare with your competitors?

Your Capabilities...
Investigate their understanding of what products / services you offer and identify any potential or missed opportunities. For example, find out:
- When do they use you, and when do they use your 'competitors'?
- Are they aware of your full range of products/ services?
- Are they using somebody else for something you can do (better?)
- What % of their 'spend' is spent with you?
- Do they see the need for your products/services increasing in the future?

You also need to understand...

Their Needs, Problems & Aspirations

Identify potential opportunities by developing an understanding of the issues that face them. For example, find out:
- What are their future plans?
- What is/might stop them getting there?
- What are they looking for in a supplier?
- What disappoints them about suppliers and other businesses like you?
- Who else influences the decision to use your products/services?
- What issues face them?

And...

Them Personally
This is about building rapport, not about 'prying' or invading their privacy. Understanding an individual's personal circumstances, interests and aspirations can be a key building block in developing stronger relationships. For example:
- What's their background?
- What are their ambitions?
- What do they like to do outside of work?
- What's important to them at work?
- What motivates or inspires them?
- What 'turns them on' or 'off'?

Then What?

Your challenge is to use the information gathered to highlight future potential. For example:
- Are there mismatches in terms of your actual performance, your view of it, and the customers view?
- Are you missing out on opportunities because your customers don't know what you can do or you weren't aware that they had a need for a particular product/service?

So, 3 Questions For You...
- **How well do you know your customers?**
- **What processes do you have to get to know them?**
- **How do you 'Demonstrate' that you know them?**

An integral ingredient of Maximised Relationships is...

Dialogue, Not Diatribes

Do you have real conversations with your customers? Do you actually 'engage' with them, or are you guilty of being like many businesses and do you simply send stuff to them?

Engaging with customers is a key ingredient of the **3D** Business approach – it's all about creating 'Dialogue, Not Diatribes', having conversations with customers and establishing real 'connections' that increase loyalty and repeat business.

3D Demonstrated: Bottom's Up!

Innocent Smoothies are another great example of a 3D Business. As well as producing quality products, they consistently do things that get people talking and they create **dialogue with their customers.** One of the things they do is online competitions for their customers. One example was to come up a phrase or comment to go on the bottom of their bottles. It got a great response - the winner came up with *'Trapped in bottle factory, please send help'.*

Anyone could submit a few words (maximum 40 characters) via the 'comments' section of their website and the one that got picked got a few freebies and the glory of their comment 'up in lights' (well, on the bottom of thousands of Innocent Smoothie bottles).
As they explained *"Next thing you know, you're a published writer, and people around the country are*

> *chuckling at your words, throwing money at you and*
> *asking you to be godparent to their child and stuff.*
> *Such is the power of the hidden message."*
>
> We love the simplicity, the humour and cost
> effectiveness of it all. It's all done in a fun, quirky way
> completely in line with the 'Innocent' way of doing
> things. It creates 'dialogue' with customers, and it
> doesn't cost them anything.

As mentioned earlier, Maximising Customer
Relationships is not a one way relationship, and is not
a passive thing. Customers need to be *engaged.* That
means interacting on a personal and business level and
tailoring the experience specifically to each customer
to help 'lock them in' with the 'ties that bind'. It's about
letting customers recognise the 'personalisation'. The
more 'personalised' it feels, the more difficult it is for
competitors to get in there.

> **3D Demonstrated: Ella's Kitchen**
>
> Ella's Kitchen is a business that does this brilliantly
> and a great example of how they do it was their Big
> Taste Test which encouraged their customers to
> send in videos of their little ones "being thrilled by a
> scrummy new food to help us learn lots more about
> what tickles babies' taste buds".
>
> It's simple stuff and created a real buzz – it was very
> visible, fun and it totally reflected and reinforced the
> Ella's Kitchen brand and ethos – even better was that

it was so easy to enter. Customers simply loaded their videos up straight from their computer. The videos were entered into a competition with the winner receiving a year's supply of Ella's Kitchen food.

It's a great example of a successful business that has really 'engaged' with its customers and has established a real 'community'. Ella's Kitchen add value to their community by providing stimulating, educational and fun things such as cook books, nutritional advice, activity sheets and even Tasty Tunes - songs for little ones you can download for free about fruit and veg to help your kids eat and enjoy their greens to. As they themselves say, it's 'scrummylicious' stuff.

Our research indicates that a frequent comment from Customer Attitude Surveys carried out for many of our clients is "you don't keep us informed" or even worse "you never return our calls". Maximised Relationships require a framework for having conversations with customers. It's about finding out how they want to be kept informed – a weekly email, a fortnightly call or meeting? What works for them? It means agreeing the parameters, and sticking to them.

3D Demonstrated: PJ Taste

A **3D** business that creates dialogue with its customers very well is caterers PJ Taste. They have established themselves as local market leaders and have built up an impressive list of delighted customers for their nutritious, healthy and high, quality food. Their Dramatic Difference is that they are passionate about high quality locally sourced food and just some of the things that they do to create Dialogue and Demonstrate that passion include…

- **The PJ Taste Blog:**
You'll often read about MD Peter's 'adventures' scurrying and foraging in the local countryside for fresh produce ingredients. His passion shines through and his tips and ideas have created lots of 'raving fans'

- **Innovative Events:**
From special breakfasts in National Farmhouse Breakfast Week to a secret supper club there's always something going on – even A Night Of Wild Fungi And Beer. Again, their passion and enthusiasm is there for all to see (and experience).

- **Educating People:**
Whether it's about the joys (and benefits) of foraging and how to do it, nutritional information and advice as an integral part of their proposals when quoting to cater for an event, to their staff understanding and explaining these things to customers and demonstrating their passion at those events, this is clearly an integral element of their Dramatic Difference and adds to the whole customer experience.

Pro-active communication can take many forms; consider sending articles of interest, leads and opportunities, press cuttings, emails, highlighting a useful website, industry updates. Anything that adds value in a format that works for your customer.

Unfortunately, not everyone gets it right...

3D 'Undemonstrated': CRM? Can't Remember My Name.

We got an email through from a company promoting their CRM software solution. It extoled the virtues of Customer Relationship Management and explained that CRM is... *a business philosophy involving identifying, understanding and better providing for your customers, while building a relationship with each customer to improve customer satisfaction and maximise profits. It's about understanding, anticipating and responding to customers' needs.*

It went on to say that ... *to manage the relationship with the customer a business needs to collect the right information about its customers and organise that information for proper analysis and action. It needs to keep that information up-to-date, make it accessible to employees, and provide the knowhow for employees to convert that data into products better matched to customers' needs.*

Apparently their product will do exactly that, which all sounds great and very much worth having. However, the email then said...

This email was sent for the personal attention of 'Jean Edwards of Hallmarks Business Developement':

A couple of points....
1. **We sold our business Hallmarks Business Development 10 years ago.**
2. **There was never anyone who worked there called Jean Edwards.**
3. **'Developement' should have been 'Development'.**

No thanks.

Too many businesses believe marketing is about shouting about themselves and that communication with their customers and potential customers simply means informing or telling them. They see networking (online and offline) as getting as many 'tweets', business cards and brochures out as possible. They work on the theory that as long as their message is being 'shouted out' then people will be listening.

It's simply not true. Many of your customers, people and network contacts are likely to be switching off from your 'marketing messages'.

So what should we do about it?

3 Ideas To Create 'Dialogue' With Your Customers

1. Get 'Permission'.

In days gone by, marketing was all about whoever shouted the loudest and most often. Hence the strong power of TV, radio and newspaper advertising. The bigger the budget, the better chance you had of grabbing people's attention.

Although they can still be effective promotion methods, there's a lot of evidence that their effect is declining as we become more questioning, use an increasingly diverse range of media, and have the ability to find what we want, when we want it through the on-line world, 24/7.

Many people see advertising as intrusive and uninvited and find ways of blocking unwanted messages out. Don't believe us? Are you in the Mail Preference System to stop unwanted junk mail? Are you 'ex-directory' to prevent cold calls? Do you have 'spam filters' to block uninvited emails? What about Sky+ so you can avoid the adverts?

'Permission Marketing' is about customers 'signing up' and choosing to proactively 'engage'. (No one's forcing you to read this for example – we hope!)

Have a look at yourself – are you guilty of 'forcing' your message onto people who aren't, or who don't want to listen? Would it be better to focus on those who want to listen? In this day and age, it's clear that the 'quality' of your contacts on your database is far better than the 'quantity'.

2. Think CNN.
The messages you send out to customers and contacts can be filed under 3 basic headings:

Critical – this is stuff that's vital to them, could really help them, solve their problems and make a real difference to them. It adds value, and they would thank you for sending it to them.

Nice To Know – useful, interesting stuff, but please don't send them too much.

Noise – all the stuff they're not interested in, the irrelevant and unrequested 'guff'. Irrelevance is defined by them, the customer, by the way.

Have you worked out what's 'Critical' to your customers? How much of your marketing material is really just 'Noise'? Because as consumers we are bombarded with so much 'Noise' on a daily basis, we create 'ear defenders' to block it out. Are you 'ranting' loudly but in reality, no one is listening?

3. Create Conversations. It's about having
'conversations' with your customers, getting their opinions, thoughts and ideas. It could be something as simple as asking *'what do you think?'*

When was the last time you had a real 'conversation' with one of your customers? We don't just mean about the weather or who's going to win 'Britain's Got Talent', but meaningful stuff about your performance, their aspirations and challenges. How often do you tap into their opinions, thoughts or ideas?

So…

- **What are you doing to create 'Dialogue, Not Diatribes' with your customers?**
- **What are you doing to 'engage' them?**
- **What are you doing to 'add value' to them?**

While we're on this, try this...

Wake Up Your 'Dormant' Customers

Have you got any customers that used to buy from you, but you haven't heard from for some time – or maybe, they haven't heard from you?

Dormant customers are those that don't currently buy from you, but have done so in the past. Your challenge is to 'wake them up' - They are a massive potential opportunity – provided of course, that they are not **'Disaffected'**. They may well have thought you were good at what you do, but for whatever reason, have just 'drifted'. Why don't they buy from you anymore? That reason may well be you. Have you not contacted them for some time? Have they forgotten you were around? Has your original contact moved on? Have your competitors moved in?

3D Businesses avoid these sorts of customers by continually engaging with them via the frequency, format and channels that suit the customers.

Go on, get in touch with your **'Dormant'** Customers, re-introduce yourself, re-engage them, get them back. It's not about blatantly shouting at them, but (re) creating 'conversations'.

Here we go... more questions:
- **Who are your 'Dormant' customers?**
- **When was the last time you were in touch?**
- **What could you do to 're-engage' with them?**

12 Questions To Create That 'Dialogue'

Lots of businesses invest a lot of time, money and effort in getting customer feedback. We also think that lots of businesses waste lots of time, money and effort in getting customer feedback. Why? They ask the wrong questions, they ask lots of questions, but don't actually listen, or they listen to the answers and then do nothing about what they hear.

We're all for getting customer feedback – it's a great source of ideas, opportunities, improvements, and it demonstrates to your customers you care (provided of course you do listen and then take action).

Too many businesses simply get boxes ticked, 'go through the motions', and ask questions that don't make them too uncomfortable. So, just to get you thinking, here are 12 questions you might want to consider asking your customers.

These questions are not the 'traditional' customer feedback questions that typically get asked, and we're not suggesting that you ask them all to everyone of your customers. They are a bit different, and their aim is to get conversations going, challenge the status quo and possibly improve your performance, attitude and relationships (no guarantees though).

1. **What attracted you to us originally?** This helps get a view of how you are seen in the market place and what the things are, that appeal to your customers.

2. **What would you do if we weren't here?** This may give an insight into the value they place on you as a supplier. Would they actually notice?

3. **Can you name one particular individual who has impressed you in our business?** This highlights your customer champions, and maybe some of your 'unsung heroes'. If they can't name anyone, what does that say about the way your people interact with your customers?

4. **What one thing could we do better?** Just one thing – it may highlight their priorities and key issues.

5. **Why do you buy from us?** This highlights your strengths, some of which, you may not be aware of. (Be careful how you phrase this one. You might sound as if you're doubting yourselves if you say it wrong).

6. **If Carlsberg ran our business, what would it look like?** You know the adverts – this one 'stretches the imagination', and even though you may not be able to 'deliver' exactly what they say, it may give you a few ideas about what they see as important.

7. **Name one thing that we do or don't do that irritates or annoys you.** This one speaks for itself. The key is doing something about it.

8. **Who can we learn from?** This helps you identify who your customers see as 'role models', and might just point something out that's not happening in your business that you could learn from.

9. **What would you say to someone else who asked you about us?** Their initial response to this is often a revealing one.

10. **What is the one thing we should never stop doing?** This one tells you what they really value about you.

11. **Are you 'completely' happy with us?** It can only be answered 'yes' or 'no'. It's a brave question, but it stops us rationalising away when people score us a 7 or 8 when we ask them to rate us out of 10. The obvious follow up question is ...

12. **Why / Why not?**

You may feel you can't ask these questions to your customers. That's not a problem, but why not find some questions that you can ask? So, go on, ask some questions, listen to the responses and do something as a result. What have you got to lose?

The 3 key factors in securing customer loyalty to small businesses....

- **A warm greeting and a smile – 59%**
- **Brilliant customer service – 36%**
- **Remembering their usual order – 22%**

60% of customers said that they would be prepared to pay more for a product from a small business that delivered this rather than a large corporate enterprise

The Small Business Research Centre at Kingston University

Only 54% of businesses say that they made a practice of doing these things.

Are You?

.......Keep smiling.

3D Demonstrated: Conrad Hotels – Personalising The Experience.

Imagine getting back to your hotel after your early morning jog and your breakfast is there waiting for you just how you like it. Imagine arranging your airport pick up just by tapping on your iPad as you land. Imagine getting the pillows you want via your smartphone.

Well, The Conrad Concierge App will help you do just that. It's their 'Dramatically and Demonstrably Different' approach to creating a personalised customer experience. The 'app' integrates with the booking and management systems of their 20 hotels worldwide and with a few simple clicks, users can manage a range of services including room service, transportation, local attractions, spa appointments, housekeeping requests, wakeup calls and more – and it can do so in 13 different languages.

They are a great example of identifying what customers want and then responding.

Research by Conrad showed that nearly 75% of consumers use a smartphone, tablet or computer when booking elements of their travel, and that 77% of traveller's value service when selecting a hotel. Additionally, nearly 70% of U.S. travellers prefer hotels that can customize their experience to reflect their personal desires and anticipate their needs.

It's also clearly targeted at a specific group of

customers (Choose 'Em Or Lose 'Em) "Conrad guests represent a new generation of global travellers for whom life, business and pleasure seamlessly interact," said John Vanderslice, Global Head of Luxury and Lifestyle Brands at Hilton Worldwide. *"Conrad Concierge allows for this interaction by putting the control in the hands of our guests. Whether it's scheduling a wake-up call while you're at a business dinner or booking a relaxing spa treatment, this new app offering allows for a seamless and intuitive experience".*

It's a great example of using technology to create a 'personalised customer experience'.

Technology's good, but it doesn't have to be 'all modern'...

Don't 'Write Off' The Old Fashioned Ways

The average UK worker sends and receives 10,000 emails a year and 25% of UK workers don't remember life without email. That's just two statistics that paint an interesting picture of today's 'modern' workplace.

A report by Warwick Business School highlights that the average UK worker now sends and receives 40 emails a day and 1 in 12 deal with a 100 plus emails each day. 57% of us log in outside of work and 85% of those who do it think it makes them more productive.

What is interesting is the decline in 'traditional' methods of communication with
- **20% of us never putting pen to paper**
- **10% of us never making phone calls and**
- **48% of us never posting a letter.**

It's clear evidence of a rapidly changing world, and it has a number of interesting of implications for us all in business – one of which is perhaps the 'old fashioned' personalised, handwritten letter might actually be a **3D** way of communicating and standing out from the crowd.

E mail is so easy. E mail newsletters are relatively easy too... and cheap. We can all reach our customers quickly, efficiently and economically at the press of a few keys on the pc. As a result, there's little or no differentiation. So the downside is 'bland' reinforcement - email templates that everyone uses, and anyone being able to 'have a go at it' (sending something that looks good is not a substitute for something that is good!).

Of course, email and e-newsletters have their place and can be a very effective and useful tool for many of the reasons we've outlined above (our own email newsletter creates opportunities and enquiries for us, so we know it works), but the danger is we come to rely on it – we tick the box that says we've contacted our customers this month, and leave it at that.

In these tougher times when everyone is at it and when customer relationships are a key factor for success, maybe it's time to do something 'Dramatically and Demonstrably Different'. It may not be fashionable in this age of 24/7 'instant' communication, but why not write your customers a personalised letter or send them a card?

These things can demonstrate that you care, because they require effort. They show that you've thought about it, taken some time out to do it and, when it's personalised, come across as something genuine and meaningful.

Here are some basic pointers to getting this right:
- The note should appear spontaneous or unexpected (as we've shown you earlier, you can in fact plan 'spontaneity')
- It needs to be 'personalised' – to a named individual, with relevant content that relates to something specific about them or their business
- It should be 'unconditional' – don't try to sell something else, or introduce a new product or service, no matter how subtle
- Handwritten works best – it reinforces the personalisation

- Create a reason for the note – 'congratulations', 'well done' or even a simple 'thank you' counts
- Be genuine – don't 'creep' or overdo it
- Keep it simple and to the point.

Let's get this straight. Personal notes don't replace email, and are no substitute for spreading a mass message. They are not usually suitable for day to day correspondence in a fast paced global business world.

They can be a way of demonstrating a difference. See them as an 'extra', an 'addition to', a genuine attempt to 'touch' your customers and to 'personalise' your relationships. They may be 'old fashioned', but we all like to be recognised as human beings. Personal notes can remind us that someone took time out to do just that.

Sometimes, doing things the 'old ways' make us stand out from the crowd. Why? Because everyone else has simply forgotten how to do it.

So, don't 'write off' those old fashioned ways, simply 'write off'.

Maximise Relationships - Think 'Share Of Customer'

The 'giving the best to' aspect of Maximising Customer Relationships is the stuff we've talked a lot about so far: the 'remarkable' customer service, the speedy response, the flexibility, the personal touch, you know, showing customers you care. The 'getting the best from' is the payback. It's the repeat business, the loyalty, the recommendations, referrals, and ultimately, the increased spend. Unfortunately, many businesses don't take a proactive approach to make this happen – do you?

A pro-active approach to spotting and maximising opportunities is an integral ingredient of Maximising Customer Relationships. A key principle is that people buy from people and organisations that they like, trust and have high expectations of. In simple terms, 'maximising' opportunities is the pay off.

Research indicates that in the UK it typically costs six to ten times more to sell to a new customer than it does to an existing one. It never fails to amaze us how many businesses seem obsessed with chasing new ones rather than putting time and effort into 'maximising' existing ones.

3D Demonstrated: Amazon - MCR in Action.
Amazon is often highlighted as the number one brand when it comes to customer service. For example The Temkin Group asked 6000 customers to rate their customer experience and Amazon came out top with 81% rating them 'good' or 'excellent'.

How do they do it? Well, there are no 'magical answers', but they do demonstrate the ingredients of MCR

Amazon ....
- **Are 'Easy To Buy From' – Although there's an incredible array of goods, the thing you need is easy to find and the process of ordering and buying it is pain free too with 'One-Click'**
- **'Delight' You – They deliver things before the date advertised and keep you updated about progress**
- **'Personalise' Things – Those emails that keep you informed and tell you what's going on don't appear 'robotised'**
- **'Remember' You – They know what you bought last time**
- **'Educate' You - They 'make recommendations' based on previous purchases – that creates more sales (that's the 'maximise' bit)**
- **'Do It Consistently' Day in, day out.......That's the key bit...**

These are all 'simple' things we know - not simple we suspect for a $34 Billion business, but if they can do it, then surely there's hope for us all.

THINK IN 3D... THE 7 CHARACTERISTICS OF 'DRAMATICALLY AND DEMONSTRABLY DIFFERENT' BUSINESSES

Often, businesses have customers who are unaware of all the products or services that they offer. The challenge is to 'educate' them. This does not mean blatantly 'pushing' products or services at them. The key is to ensure relevance. It's **not** about simply mass mailing company 'propaganda'. It's about keeping it brief, keeping it interesting and keeping it relevant.

3D Demonstrated...

Andy was at his local gym (honest) and saw something that he found really useful for him as a customer. It was a graph on the wall that highlighted occupancy / attendance levels by members each day by the hour. It showed the busy times and the quiet times and did a number of things really well:
- It makes it 'easier' for him as a customer to utilise their resources
- It 'manages his expectations' in terms of 'busyness' and waiting times
- It 'educates' him to help him get the best out of their service

We suspect it also helps them to manage their own resources better too by ensuring staff are aware of customer levels. It's a nice example of giving the best to, and getting the best from, their customers.

How effective are **you** at educating your customers?

A referral is significantly more powerful than a cold call. Are you leveraging the relationships with your 'devoted' customers?

'Devoted' customers tell others - some even become 'evangelists' and spread the word at every opportunity. Who else in the customer's organisation or network has a need or use for your products and services? The best businesses develop a pro-active approach at finding out and leveraging the relationship. Sometimes it's as simple as just asking.

3D Demonstrated: Charity: Water

Charity: Water have developed an innovative approach to leveraging their relationships. They engage their fundraisers via **The Birthday** initiative. Rather than receive presents, you ask family and friends to donate money equivalent to your birthday age to the charity. Again, it's simple to do and is a great way of spreading the word – people post and share their campaigns. **Over $9 million has been raised so far** by this fun and unique approach - **the average birthday pledge campaign raises $770** and as Charity: Water point out, **this helps an average of 38 people each time.** The visible and engaging approach gets more revenue from their existing 'customers' and encourages lots and lots of referrals and recommendations.

Maximising Opportunities, Not Missing Them

Here are a couple of simple ideas to help you **M**aximise Customer **R**elationships – one 'strategic', the other quite 'tactical'. Establish what works for you:

Idea 1 - Think 'share of customer', not 'share of market'

This is about looking at individual customers' spend with you as a % of their total spend on the sort of products and services that you provide. We don't mean to the minute detail, but is it high or low? Do you actually know how much they spend on them each year (with you and totally)?

For example, do you know those who spend a lot each year and the vast majority of it is with you? These clearly are your KEY customers – what are you doing to get and keep close?

KEEP IN TOUCH with those who don't spend much, but when they do, they come to you – maintain dialogue, remind them you're there (by adding value, not 'unwanted marketing rants'). Educate them too – can you increase their spend?

Those that don't spend much and don't come to you, KEEP AWAY. Remember 'Choose 'em or lose 'em'. What about those who spend a lot overall each year, but only a small % comes to you? Por QUE? 'Why' is that? Are you close enough to them? Are they aware of the full range of what you can offer? How could you increase that %?

We worked with one business that broke their regular pattern and spent one monthly sales meeting reviewing their customers spend with them as a % of their total spend. Some they knew well, but many were in a 'Don't Know' category. They agreed to clarify this for the next meeting by talking to and listening to their customers. The outcomes were surprising and identified masses of missed opportunities. The number of customers who simply were not aware of the full range of products they provided, and the number of high spending customers that they had been 'ignoring' was scary. By drawing up simple MCR plans for the customers with potential, and, vitally, delivering on those plans, within 3 months the results were amazing.

Idea 2 - Selling Up and Selling On

This is about having systems and processes that

help you and your people look for and develop new opportunities with your customers. Sometimes it is simply about maximising the transaction that you're engaged in.

3D Demonstrated: 5 Little Words

Jill had an interesting experience some years ago when she was waiting for a train that had been delayed. She decided to have a cup of coffee. The guy selling it to her asked *"Fancy a danish with that?"* *"Go on then"* she said, and paid him. She sat down, enjoying her coffee and danish, and watched him. He made everyone feel comfortable as he served them, and he also asked lots of people casually *"Fancy a danish with that?"* Some took it up and some didn't.

Jill went up to him and asked if he'd been trained to do that. He explained that it was his own franchise business, and he just did it to maximise opportunities. She asked him if he'd be kind enough to take her through the figures. Each danish cost him 25p, he sold them for 75p. He reckoned that he sold about 40 extra in a day - he'd been monitoring it. That was £20 'extra' profit a day, on five days a week that was £100 a week and therefore £5,000 a year 'extra' profit a year from 5 little words.

The point is this. That was his simple system to maximise opportunities. He very quickly built a 'relationship' with his customers and introduced them to an additional product. No hard sell, no big deal if they said 'no', but systematically asking the question.

What's your strategy and systems for maximising opportunities with your customers? As a minimum, please don't ever let happy existing customers walk away when they want to spend money.

3D Demonstrated: Tell / Sell

An engineering distribution business developed a tell/sell approach to its customer base. The sales team from the whole business got together to evaluate a group of targeted customers and established which customers knew about each product group. If they did know about it, they filled in the appropriate 'T' for 'Tell' section to acknowledge this. If they felt the customer was unaware of the specific product then the section was left empty and these customers were prioritised for future promotional activity aimed at 'educating' them, and raising product awareness. They then identified which customers were actually buying each product group and this would be marked with an 'S' for 'Sell'. By reviewing these each month, they developed a proactive approach to maximising opportunities with their customers.

Maximising Customer Relationships is a 'way of doing things'. It's a philosophy. It's an attitude. And, it's one that is shared at every level of the business and drives performance. It looks different in every business, and there are no simple 'lists' of things to do, or 'rules' to follow.

Your challenge is to create a focused approach to developing and maximising relationships with your customers. It starts with 'establishing' who your iDeal customers are (the ones you want) and what they want, and what they think... and keep doing that.

It's about focus, it's about planning and it's about proactivity...

A One Page Guide To Help Focus Your Efforts

Here's a one page guide to focusing your time, resources and efforts on your customers...

Disinterested customers...   Stay away.

iDeal customers...   Get more.

Detached customers...   Exceed their expectations.

Delighted customers...   Do it consistently.

Devoted customers....   Maximise them.

Disappointed customers...   Spot and deal with them.

Disaffected customers...   Show them you've done it.

Dormant customers...   Re-engage them

Draining customers...   Dump them.

Dumped customers...   Good, keep them there.

One last thing...

DO SOMETHING!

So, before we move on to #Characteristic 5… Let's take a minute to reflect on #Characteristic 4:

- **What does a Maximised Customer Relationship look like for you?**

- **How do your current relationships measure up?**

- **What do your customers think?**

"Selling to people who actually want to hear from you is more effective than interrupting strangers who don't"

Seth Godin

THINK IN 3D... THE 7 CHARACTERISTICS OF 'DRAMATICALLY AND DEMONSTRABLY DIFFERENT' BUSINESSES

8. 3D Characteristic # 5:
Create An UBER Culture.

The 7 'Characteristics' of 3D Businesses are:

#1: Get That Vision Thing!

#2: Think in **3D**!

#3: Create Delighted and Devoted Customers

#4: Forget CRM – Think MCR:
'*Maximise* Customer Relationships'

#5: Create an UBER Culture

#6: KeeP In Control

#7: InnovatiON!

This chapter will look at how you

#Create an UBER Culture

"The one thing that I have learned at IBM is that culture is everything"

Louis V. Gerstner, Jr. former CEO IBM

When It Comes To Creating An UBER Culture, Here Are 10 Things We See 3D Businesses Doing

They…

1. Establish It…
They work hard at creating and establishing the culture they want and need to support their 'Dramatic Difference'.

2. Create Understanding…
They ensure that everyone understands what's expected of them when it comes to 'the way we do things around here'.

3. Value Their Values…
They create and live a set of values that shape and reinforce their behaviours.

4. Make It Tangible…
They clearly and consistently spell out their 'core values' – not lots of nice posters on the wall, but 'preferred behaviours' that can 'be lived in the day to day'.

5. Build Systems And Processes…
They establish systems and processes that help shape and reinforce their culture – from recruiting people that 'fit' to reward systems that reinforce the 'preferred behaviours' they want.

6. Engage…
They ensure that everyone in the business 'buys in' to the culture and they keep it 'alive'.

7. Empower...
They provide their people with guidelines and permission to 'make things happen'.

8. Enable...
They give them the training, knowledge and support to do this.

9. Champion Their Champions...
They reward and recognise those that live and demonstrate the behaviours they want.

10. Challenge Their Challengers...
They challenge those that don't.

What Exactly Is Culture?

Culture is often seen as the 'soft' or 'touchy feely' side of business. Our experience suggests it's actually the hardest. Why? Because it deals with attitudes and behaviours which all somehow seem a bit vague, and can be hard to manage. It's much easier to talk about territories, product life cycles, sales targets, margins and advertising budgets - they're 'real' and 'tangible'.

In fact, in reality, culture is very tangible. As customers we often experience the 'culture' of a business simply by talking to and interacting with employees, whether it's by email, on the telephone or face to face. In **3D** Businesses 'culture' is an integral part of the 'Dramatic Difference', and it is not left to chance.

But what exactly is culture? Our very simple definition of 'culture' in a business is -

'The way we do things around here'

(simple we know, but that's how we like it!). Another definition we love is by Herb Kelleher, the former CEO of Southwest Airlines, which we thinks builds on this. He says culture is

'What people do when no-one is looking'

We love that! Southwest Airlines spell this out to their employees, by expecting and encouraging them to be themselves in everything they do, and this reinforces their 'Dramatic Difference'. In fact you could argue, it is their 'Dramatic Difference'.

And an **UBER** culture is one that creates real competitive advantage, that attracts both customers and employees, and gives them reasons to stay and to tell others.

Our research suggests that the key ingredients of an **UBER** culture are:

- **Everyone Understands what's expected of them and behaves accordingly and consistently as a result**
- **Systems and processes are Built to reinforce the 'preferred behaviours'**
- **People are Engaged, Empowered and Encouraged to act in line with them**
- **People are Rewarded and Recognised for doing it.**

This chapter highlights these ingredients and provides some questions to help you see how you and your business 'measures up'.

But first of all...

Culture? Why Bother?

According to a Deloitte report in 2013 it states that 94% of executives and 88% of employees believe a distinct workplace culture is important to business success. This is reinforced by the *Employee Engagement Task Force Report, Headed by David Macleod and Nita Clarke* which found…

The top 25% 'most engaged' companies enjoy the benefits of:
- **200% higher annual net profit**
- **18% higher productivity**
- **250% revenue growth**
- **12% greater customer advocacy**
- **50% fewer sick days**
- **87% less likely to leave organisation**
  … compared with the lowest 25%

However, it's not just about it being important. Deloitte's report goes on to say…

"Exceptional organizations have core beliefs that are unique, simple, leader- led, repetitive, and embedded in the culture. There is a correlation between clearly articulated and lived culture and strong business performance".

So, you see... this 'culture stuff' is not just about being 'touchy – feely'.

3D Demonstrated: HubSpot

HubSpot is a company that develops and markets a software-as-a-service product for inbound marketing. The business was set up by Brian Halligan and Dharmesh Shah in 2006.

Like many businesses, initially culture wasn't always something that they focused on: *"In the early years of HubSpot we didn't talk about culture at all,"* Dharmesh explained on Inc.com. Then he started working intensely on building and developing the culture of his business that focuses on customer delight, and it clearly seems to be working – the inbound marketing company has grown from a $2 million business in 2008 to over $52 million today.

Dharmesh explains; *"A couple of years ago I started a simple document that talked a bit about culture, describing the kinds of people that seemed to do well at HubSpot and that we wanted to recruit. Then I started getting feedback from the team that it wasn't going far enough: It described the who, but didn't address any of the how or why."*

Part of this involved developing 7 principles that shape and drive the culture of the business; these are a brilliant example of **3D Thinking**. However, it's not just about the 7 principles. They've established systems and processes that support and reinforce the culture of this incredibly fast growing business. These include...
- Sharing (almost) everything. They protect

> information only that they are legally required to do and when it's not completely theirs to share (salary details for example)
> - An in-house Wiki site that shares financial information, and details of Board and Senior Management meetings
> - A seat shuffle every 3 months (which they say, reflects the fact that change is constant)
> - Unlimited free books for personal development
> - Unlimited free meals to get to know your colleagues
> - A 3 word policy on just about everything; such as social media policy, sick day policy, travel policy, working from home policy, 'buy a round of drinks at an event policy' and that 3 word policy is…
>
> ………………'USE GOOD JUDGEMENT'.

Hopefully, you can see here that Hubspot didn't just come up with asset of values and leave it at that. They made them meaningful. Here's how Innocent Smoothies spell out their values…

> ### 3D Demonstrated: Innocent Smoothies
>
> The guys who set up Innocent Smoothies wanted to create a business they could be proud of. To make this happen they believed that they need 'brilliant people who inspire and deliver change all around them'. That's why they're always looking for talented, ambitious, and altruistic people to join them. They work hard on the culture and have a set of 'core values' that shape the 'way they do things around here':

- **Be natural**
  Not just our products, but being natural in how we treat each other and how we speak to the most important people - our drinkers.

- **Be entrepreneurial**
  Innocent began as a small, entrepreneurial company, and nothing much has changed. We aren't afraid to do things differently, and we've never given up on a good opportunity.

- **Be responsible**
  We keep our promises, are mindful of our impact on our community and our environment, and always try to leave things a little bit better than we found them.

- **Be commercial**
  We wouldn't be here if we didn't keep our eyes on the numbers at all times. Ultimately we want to deliver growth for us and our customers too.

- **Be generous**
  This means giving honest feedback to one another, taking time to say thank you, and where we can, donating our resources or money to those who need it more than us. It's that simple.

So...
- Do you have a clear set of core values?
- Have you overturned the 'preferred behaviours' you want from your people?
- Do they understand and 'buy-in' to them?

So, Let's Look At The 4 Ingredients Of UBER Culture...

Ingredient 1: Everyone Understands what's expected of them and behaves accordingly and consistently as a result.

In the same way that **3D** leaders shape and communicate a 'vision', they also spell out a picture of the culture they are striving for. This can often be just a set of guiding principles or 'values', but the best seem to go further by establishing 'preferred behaviours' that support these values.

So, what's the 'value' of values?

Values can...
- define the fundamental character of a business
- create a sense of identity
- shape how we do things around here
- help determine how resources will be allocated
- reduce game playing, politics and confusion
- provide guidance for acceptable and unacceptable behaviours
- help build the brand and reputation of the business

According to Derek Irvine in his *"Revealing Key Practices for Effective Recognition"* Report, 65% of employees, who could name their values, say they had a strong grasp on company objectives, compared to only 23 % who say they didn't know any. And, 88% of those who know their core values say they are engaged compared to 54% who say they didn't know any of their company values.

Core values can help provide guidelines for acceptable and unacceptable behaviours – experience shows that this also helps manage performance more effectively. Again, getting 'ownership' of these behaviours is key. It should not just be seen as a 'management thing'.

Whatever you do, please, please don't just put stylish 'arty' posters of people rowing together 'as a team' on the wall in your reception and hope for the best that you promote 'teamwork'. Here are some examples of 'core values' from some **3D** Businesses –

3D Demonstrated: Apple's values...
- Be passionate
- Lead, don't follow
- Aim to surprise
- Be unreasonable
- Innovate incessantly
- Sweat the small details
- Think like an engineer, feel like an artist

3D Demonstrated: Zappos Values
- Deliver wow through service
- Embrace and drive change
- Create fun and a little weirdness
- Be adventurous, creative, and open-minded
- Pursue growth and learning
- Build open and honest relationships with communication
- Build a positive team and family spirit
- Do more with less
- Be passionate and determined
- Be humble

3D Demonstrated: Google's values...

1. Focus on the user and all else will follow
2. It's best to do one thing really, really well
3. Fast is better than slow
4. Democracy on the web works
5. You don't need to be at your desk to need an answer.
6. You can make money without doing evil
7. There's always more information out there
8. The need for information crosses all borders
9. You can be serious without a suit
10. Great just isn't good enough

And finally...

3D Demonstrated: Webmart's Values...

- Trusting each other as default
- Honest
- Direct
- Friendly

And...
- Fundamentally good

As MD, Simon Biltcliffe says *"Common sense Northern Principles."*

Remember it's not about copying these, they are just examples. Your challenge is to work to establish *your* values.

It's clear that this stuff doesn't happen by chance. **3D** Businesses proactively take steps that help develop an **UBER** culture which mean that they truly value their 'values'. They clarify what these values really mean to their people – the result is clear definitions of acceptable and unacceptable behaviours. They use them in the day to day management of their people, and in the recruitment and rewarding of their people. Their leaders talk about and refer to them regularly and use them consistently. They act as role models and actively promote the behaviours they want to see in others. Those that don't, simply put up those posters and talk a good story.

Remember this is about actions, not words. Apparently, Enron had a set of published values, one of which was integrity. It's not what you say, it's what you do that counts. A 5-year academic study by the 'University of Chicago of Great Place to Work' data, shows that there is a direct link between an organisation's values as perceived by its employees and its financial performance.

However, here's a health warning.

The report goes on to say…

"There is no correlation between an organisation's published values (e.g. on its website) and financial performance"

"There is a correlation between a culture of strong values ('high integrity') as perceived by employees and performance"

In other words, it's not what you say, it's what you DO, and what you are seen to be DOING.

3D businesses...

Ensure that actions match the words.

This is a critical issue. Lots of business leaders say the right things, but don't actually 'live' it. In those organisations that 'drive' this stuff, it's the leaders who are great role models. They make the 'core values' visible and talk about them at every opportunity.

They put them on the agenda at team meetings, board meetings, and corporate communications. They recognise that their people judge them not by what they say, but by what they 'do', and crucially, what they are 'seen to do'.

3D Demonstrated: Apple

Apparently more people now visit Apple's 326 stores in a single quarter than the 60 million who visited Walt Disney's four biggest theme parks last year.

How do they do it? As well as having customer friendly environments, intensive training for employees, and of course, great products, a key element of their success is the culture that they have created, and crucially that they keep reinforcing that helps deliver consistently great customer experiences.

For example, employees are told (and trained) not to sell, but rather to help customers solve problems. "Your job is to understand all of your customers' needs—some of which they may not even realize they have," one training manual says. Interestingly, employees receive no sales commissions and have no sales targets. They are actually rewarded for customer satisfaction levels.

This is just one of the key elements that gets to the 'core' ('core', geddit?) of Apple's great customer service, and gives some great insights.

Apparently Apple gives its people clear guidelines on what to do, and how to do it, when it comes to dealing with customers For example, its "steps of service" are spelt out in the acronym **APPLE**:

- Approach customers with a personalized warm welcome
- Probe politely to understand all the customer's needs
- Present a solution for the customer to take home today
- Listen for and resolve any issues or concerns
- End with a fond farewell and an invitation to return

It's simple stuff, but it certainly seems to work.

As a result, they ensure that everything in the organisation reinforces the 'preferred behaviours'.

Ingredient 2: Systems and Processes Are Built To Reinforce The Culture

Every system and process in your business does one of two things when it comes to culture; they either, support and reinforce your 'preferred' behaviours or they suppress and detract from them. What's happening in your business?

3D Demonstrated: Timpsons

Timpson's are a great example of a business that has established, and have clearly spelled out, to their people, the behaviours they expect of them when it comes to living 'the culture they want'. They have made it very simple, Timpson's don't advertise – they believe their customers do that for them, and that comes from what their people do. Employees are encouraged to....
- Look the part and put the money in the till.
- Do anything else to best serve customers.

Simple stuff, but they don't just leave this to chance...

They have Built Systems And Processes that help shape and reinforce the behaviours they want and need. These include....
- Staff being able to spend up to £500 to settle a customer complaint (without management authorisation).
- They can charge whatever you like – the price list is a guide only.

> - They recruit on 'personality' not qualifications, and
>   look for people that 'fit' the business.
>
> Other 'systems' that reinforce how the business
> values its employees include...
> - Staff getting a day off on their birthday.
> - Holiday homes available for staff to use for free,
>   and...
> - 'Dreams Come True' where staff submit their
>   'dreams' entry and once a year and a lucky few
>   have their dreams such as family reunions, dream
>   holidays and experiences fulfilled.

When we talk about systems and processes, this
includes everything from recruitment processes and
performance management systems, communication
policies, operating procedures, employee guidelines
and reward mechanisms. Here's a quote from a
business leader that really has created and sustained
an **UBER** culture – Tony Hsieh, CEO of online shoe and
clothes retailer, Zappos:

*"We interview people for culture fit. We want people who
are passionate about what Zappos is about–service. I
don't care if they're passionate about shoes."*

Part of their recruitment and induction process actually
offers 'new recruits' $3,000 to 'walk away' during the
four week induction process. They want people totally
'committed' to what they are trying to achieve and are
prepared to 'pay' them not to join. That's just one of the
things they do to reinforce their culture.

3D Demonstrated: Zappos

Some of the other things Zappos do to reinforce their culture...

- They train their people in each of their 10 core values, so that every employee has the same message and understands the behaviours needed to live the values every day.
- They interview people intensively for 'culture fit'. It's worth 50% of the criteria, and if you don't 'pass' this 'fit' then you don't get put forward for interview.
- They have specific 'behaviour based' questions that illuminate candidates 'fit' with the Zappos culture.
- Your first four weeks employment, regardless of position, involves spending time on the phone handling calls and dealing with customers.
- Pay rises come from building skills and capabilities. Employees pass 'skills tests' and receive pay rises as a result.
- Every manager is expected to spend 20% of the department's time on team building activities.
- Performance evaluations reinforce the culture and include measuring employees on their behaviours and culture fit rather than just focusing on targets.
- Employees do not work from a script and are encouraged to use their imagination to make customer happy – they do not have to ask permission from a boss to 'delight' their customers.
- Zappos produces a 'culture book' every year that contains employees comments on what it's like working there- good and bad. Anyone can get a copy by getting in touch with them.

Do Zappos live their values? Yes, they do. A couple of years ago Andy was avidly following CEO Tony Hsieh as he was blogging about the final preparations for his book launch 'Delivering Happiness', (it's well worth a read – see later for other recommendations). The day came, and Tony presented in New York announcing that the book was available on Amazon. Andy eagerly went to the website only to see that it wasn't available in the UK yet. He emailed Tony's office to find out when it would be available and his secretary emailed back saying they'd be in touch. Two days later, Andy walked into his office to find an Amazon package on his desk and opened it, discovered a copy of the book with a 'post it' note on the front saying *"Hi Andy, hope this 'delivers you some happiness'." (Note: he has subsequently bought over 20 copies of the book to give to clients and friends).*

If you're really serious about this stuff, then you need to **B**uild it into your reward systems, feedback systems, appraisal processes, promotion criteria, recruitment and selection processes. For example, do you currently look for evidence of 'matches' to your 'core values' in prospective employees?

3D Demonstrated: Amy's Ice Creams

Amy Simmons set up Amy's Ice Creams in 1984 and she looks for creative people to do these amazing things. How do they find them? Well, they have a fairly unique application process; forget filling in forms, their process involves a white paper bag.

Applicants are encouraged to be creative with the bag
as their application for the job. They have included
decorated bags, short stories and videos placed
in the bag. Some applications have included only
portions of the bag, puppets made from the bag, or
the remains of the bag (ashes). The end product
does not need to resemble the original bag. The
only requirements are to write a name and contact
information somewhere on the application. Now,
THAT is Dramatically and Demonstrably Different.

UBER culture also means ensuring that the systems
and processes help and encourage people do what they
are supposed to do, rather than hinder them and hold
them back by 'following procedures'. Of course there
should be 'procedures', but they should reinforce the
'preferred behaviours' that you want.

3D Demonstrated: Mind Candy

Mind Candy is an incredibly successful innovative fast growth business founded in 2003 by Michael Acton Smith and has seen amazing growth over recent years. The major reason for that huge growth came in 2007 with the creation of Moshi Monsters, a virtual world and online game aimed at children aged between 6-12, which allows them to adopt their own pet monster, socialise, and play educational puzzles.

They have more than 80 million registered users today and the momentum is continuous, growing at a rate of one new user per second. This growth has come both online, and offline, with a range of physical products including toys, books, membership cards, trading cards, Top Trumps, and Plush Toys.

Under Michael's leadership the business seems to be well on track to achieve an ambitious 'vision' to be "the largest entertainment brand in the world for this new digital generation of kids". He now has a team of 200 at their 'trendy' offices in London, and a key ingredient of their success appears to be the focus on establishing and maintaining their culture.

In an article on racounteur.net he explained why:

"When I left university I did some temping jobs and worked in a lot of different companies. But they were all so boring, no one seemed to be enjoying themselves. Everywhere had the same blue carpet and strip lighting. I thought then that, if I ever had my

own business, I would create an environment that people actually liked working in".

Michael believes that one of the most important things are that people want more than just a job. In a fast moving company in a very, very competitive space, he says he wants people who really care about their careers and who are specialists in their field. *"They have to be able to do the job, that's a given. But beyond that we look for various traits – people who are passionate, playful, respectful and have the ability to think commercially."*

How does he find them? Well they have built some simple recruitment systems and processes…

As part of the recruitment process, interviewees have to do a presentation and tell their story: who they are, what they're passionate about. They look for evidence that they go beyond their jobs to sharpen their skills – do they attend conferences, or read books, or are there particular blogs that they like? Michael believes that this allows them to see whether someone is really passionate about their role.

However, he recognises that you can only learn so much about somebody in the interview process. *"During the probation period we try to figure out whether new employees are right for us and vice versa. We're a bit of an unusual place, so it doesn't work for everyone. We certainly don't have a 100 % record when it comes to hiring, but we get it right a lot more often than not."*

They work hard on reinforcing their culture. Their highly acclaimed studio looks like a Moshified playground, complete with tree-house and astro-turf, and it's designed to be a fun and inspiring place to work. Michael explains their approach:

"You arrive at Mind Candy and you smile, you're inspired by stuff on the wall, there's bizarre furniture. I don't think you need to spend a lot of money doing that, but it creates a wonderful environment. But culture is more than aesthetics. It's the events the company puts on for its staff, the way they're treated – with respect and transparent communication. We spend a lot of time trying to get that right."

Do you have a customer complaints procedure? Many businesses do. When a complaint comes in the 'official' procedure kicks in; meetings, audits, reports to senior managers, non-compliance reports, internal investigations, reviews, debriefs, corrective actions. Of course, it's all important stuff, and I'd never criticise a business for doing it.

The problem with most businesses is how they deal with a 'customer praise', if they do at all. Very rarely is it met with the same level of response, energy or formality. In many companies, at best, the letter gets put on the staff notice board, and that's that.

If you're serious about creating a customer focused culture, a greater fanfare is often needed for when stuff goes well. We all know that praise and recognition works - but too often, it's not formalised. A 'customer praise' procedure can just help do that.

3D Demonstrated: Establish A Customer Praise Procedure

An insurance business client of ours introduced a 'customer praise' procedure. They...

1. Gave someone responsibility for it. An individual formally reviewed all positive comments that came in via their customer feedback forms and made sure that they got acknowledged.

2. Put 'Customer Praise' on the agenda – they made sure that their 'customer champions' got mentioned in team meetings, and all internal communication. Team leaders were tasked with highlighting them (it was made clear that any manager consistently failing to nominate anyone was probably not leading them properly).

3. Made it public – At the end of the year they held an 'Oscars' ceremony that recognised some great individual performances from the past year. All voted by their peers, the winners included 'The Individual Who Made The Biggest Customer Impact', 'The Most Customer Focused' and 'The Biggest Unsung Hero'. (We're not suggesting that you have to have a big ceremony, but could you FORMALLY recognise your outstanding employees somehow?)

4. Got their customers to help - They asked their customers to highlight their 'customer champions' and nominate their 'outstanding' performers.

> **5. 'Championed Their Champions'** – Every month they 'rewarded' staff at all levels and departments who had 'gone the extra mile' for their customers – both internally and externally. Small rewards, but it was the recognition that worked

The example above was successful and did a number of things:

- It demonstrated the importance of great customer service (both to staff and customers)
- It reinforced the behaviours they wanted
- It highlighted brilliant performers
- It 'engaged' customers

(Very) Importantly, it increased customer satisfaction levels and repeat business levels.

Why not look at introducing a 'customer praise' process to your business?

What you do, and how you do it is up to you, but as ever, do something.

Your Signs Say A Lot Too

As well as all the 'sophisticated' recruitment and induction processes simple things like your signs in and out of businesses often say a lot about the 'culture' of your business. They reinforce key messages to customers and staff, both good and bad, and consciously and unconsciously.

3D Demonstrated: Street Food Chef

We came across a great example from a forward thinking business called Street Food Chef. It was a sign in their restaurant for all to see and that said...

"We want to take our great team out to thank them for all their hard work. SO, we will be closed on Sunday 6th April from, 7pm. We are sorry for the inconvenience, but we believe that valuing and investing in our team is key to our business."

We think it does a number of things...
- **It politely informs customers of what's going on.**
- **It shows they care about them.**
- **It shows that they care about their staff.**
- **It publically recognises their staff**
- **It makes the staff feel valued.**
- **It reinforces the importance they put both on their customers and their staff.**

Malmaison Hotels for example use signs to reinforce their 'personality'. They have some wonderful little touches. Instead of 'Do Not Disturb' signs for your door, they have 'I want to be alone', the heated towel rails say *'Keep off The Rails – be careful, they're extremely hot'*. When you order your chips with your meal the bowl they came in has *'for your fries only'* on it. It's cheesy, but fun. It makes customers smile, and appears to treat them as human beings, and dare we say it, as 'adults' with a sense of humour? It reinforces the 'culture' of the business, both to the customers and the staff.

All this is backed up with courteous, friendly and caring staff by the way which is key – Signs alone, of course, do nothing.

Signs can also reinforce 'negative' behaviours. For example, Andy once accidentally walked into the staff room of a restaurant rather than the gents and saw a note on a white board next to all the weekly figures saying *'well done guys, we really screwed those customers this week'*. What message does that send to staff?

Please note, for signs read emails, memos, meetings, and every other way you communicate with your people and your customers. Have a look at your business – what 'messages' are you sending to your people that reinforce your culture, both positively and negatively?

For example, look at how Metro Bank reinforce their culture with clear 'rules' -

3D Demonstrated: Metro Bank

Some of the key messages they spread...

- 'Buy in or opt out'. They set very clear expectations for their people that say if this isn't for you, no worries – see you.
- One person to say 'yes', two people to say 'no'. That's all about 'empowerment'.
- A 'No 'stupid rules' rule which encourage staff to challenge the things that don't work.
- Staff rewards are linked to customer service levels, not sales. That's a powerful message.

Ingredient 3: People are Engaged, Empowered and Encouraged to act in line with the 'preferred behaviours'

'Encouragement and Empowerment' are key ingredients of an **UBER** culture and here's a great example that hopefully illustrates the point, and it comes from one of our favourites – First Direct Bank.

3D Demonstrated: First Direct

A client told us a great story that she had left her office in Leeds to go to London for a couple of days. Having got there, she discovered that she had lost her purse (or it had been stolen). Understandably, she quickly got on the phone to the various banks to cancel her cards and explained that it all went very well; details taken, courteous staff and cards cancelled – no problem.

She then called First Direct, and was asked 'How are you feeling?' which was a nice start, and then the card cancellation process got underway – very similar to all the other card providers. At the end of the process, the First Direct lady then asked 'What are you going to do for money in the next couple of days if you have no purse or cards?'

'I'm not really sure' came the reply. 'Well, would you like for me to arrange £200 to be collected from a nearby HSBC bank? I've worked out where the nearest branch to your hotel is. If you tell me what you'll be wearing, I'll get them to look out for you in

---

the morning and you can collect your money.'

We're sure that there isn't a rule book at First Direct that says 'in the event of a client losing their card and being stuck in a hotel with no money, please follow this procedure'. First Direct has created a customer focused culture that encourages and 'empowers' its people to 'delight' their customers.

No wonder they are the UK's 'most recommended' bank.

An **UBER** culture doesn't happen by chance - it needs driving, managing and consistently reinforcing. Here's a great quote from Simon F Cooper, the president of Ritz Carlton Hotels that illustrates this:

"We entrust every single Ritz-Carlton staff member, without approval from their general manager, to spend up to $2,000 on a guest, and that's not per year, it's per incident".

3D Demonstrated: The Story of Joshie The Giraffe

When Chris Hurn's family came back from their holiday at the Ritz-Carlton on Amelia Island in Florida they unfortunately returned without Joshie The Giraffe, Chris's young son's 'best friend'. They'd left him behind, and as you can imagine this caused huge stress and problems sleeping.

Chris explained that there was nothing to worry about and that Joshie was having a little extra holiday and that he was fine. His son seemed to accept this and dropped off to sleep.

That evening the Ritz-Carlton called to say that they had found Joshie in the laundry and that he had been handed over to the hotel's Loss Prevention Team. Chris told them about his 'little white lie' about Joshie's extra holiday and wondered if they would mind taking a picture of Joshie on a chair by the pool to 'prove' it. To Chris's relief they said they would – so now that's two people who could sleep sound.

A couple days later a package arrived. In it was Joshie, along with some Ritz-Carlton-branded "goodies" including a frisbee and a football. Also included in the package was a binder that meticulously documented Joshie's extended stay at the hotel.

It included wonderful photographs of Joshie sunbathing by the pool, having a massage at the spa, meeting with other 'cuddly friends' and even driving down to the beach in a buggy. It also showed Joshie working on the security cameras making sure that other things didn't get lost.

It's an imaginative response from employees who are truly 'empowered' to make this stuff work.

Now, THAT'S Empowerment.

Engagement is key. That means that people understand, own and live the 'preferred behaviours' and are Encouraged to do so. There are proven links between high levels of employee engagement and higher levels of productivity, staff retention, customer loyalty and profitability and that's why this stuff is so critical.

It's all about training and developing people in 'the areas that count' and it's about encouraging them to 'deliver'. Our friends at Timpson's recognise this.

3D Demonstrated: Timpsons

Having spelt out the 'preferred behaviours' they want, they do all they can to help their staff 'deliver' them. This includes establishing clear guidelines, policies and procedures that help make this happen.

For example...
- Their staff manuals aren't just lots of words, but illustrations that staff are encouraged (and incentivised) to take home to absorb.
- It's also about giving them the knowledge and training to make that happen.
- Their customer service training sessions involve people actually going out to buy things and reflecting on and learning from, their experiences.

Another business who does this well is Pret A Manger. Pret A Manger are a successful business in the UK and are expanding fast in the US. They attribute their success to their people, and particularly, how they manage and engage them. Our experience suggests that their food is a factor too.

3D Demonstrated: Pret A Manger

Some of the things they do…
- **Ensure Behaviours Count** – Preferred attitudes and behaviours are spelt out and new hires are encouraged to 'not hide your true character'. Employees are rewarded and promoted for things like 'cheerfulness'.
- **Rewards** are also given to the whole team for 'outstanding' customer experiences spotted by weekly 'mystery shoppers'.
- **Recognise it's 'About Team'** – Rewards are for team performances, as well as individuals. For example a 'star' individual may well receive a £50 bonus for achieving a certain standard, but this has to be passed on to colleagues and people who have helped them achieve.
- **Engage Their People** – New employees are 'voted' in or out by existing staff after a 6 hour onsite shift. 90% are voted 'in' and those that aren't are paid £35 for their time.

Ingredient 4: Reward and Recognise people for doing it

Almost a third of employees in UK small and medium sized businesses admit to holding back because they feel their bosses don't value extra effort.

According to a report from BUPA, 29% admitted to doing this, and 38% admitted to 'daydreaming' and wasting time, because they are not fully engaged.

How does this impact on businesses? Well, it can be very serious. The research, which asked 2,700 employees, highlights that nearly a quarter (24%) do not try to win new business because it will mean more work for them. Now, THAT'S scary stuff.

A frustrated business leader explained how she was struggling to get her people to 'delight' their customers. *"What's the reward for doing that in your business?"* Jill asked. She looked puzzled. Talking to her staff it was clear that the 'Reward' for putting the effort in and 'going the extra mile' for a customer was lots more work.

We see it in lots of businesses, where the reward for 'going the extra mile' and 'doing a great job' is 'more work'. Do you have someone in your team that if you want a job doing well, you give it to them? Even worse, do 'slackers' get away with things?

The problem is many companies say they are doing it, but really are only giving it lip service and doing it badly.

Ever had someone in your team who achieves all

their goals and hits all their targets, but is basically a real 'pain' because they wind others up, de-motivate colleagues and upset team members? If you measure individuals on results alone, regardless of their behaviours, then you may well be asking for trouble.

3D Demonstrated: Timpsons

At Timpsons…
- Weekly bonuses are paid to all staff based on the profitability of the store they work in and it's very clear and transparent how this works.
- Staff receive a higher proportion of the weekly bonus based on the training and development courses that they have attended and completed – According to Chairman John Timpson, the result is "staff pleading to attend Health & Safety courses."
- They proactively 'Champion their Champions' by sending personalised notes to individuals who've done great stuff (at their home address and sometimes with a little bonus cheque in it.).

As well as creating and promoting 'role models', they 'challenge' those that don't act in line with their 'preferred behaviours' and John says that they get rid of poor performing staff quickly.

3D Businesses 'Reward' the 'behaviours' they want as well as results. This is about making it very clear to people what is expected of them, and the 'preferred behaviours' that you want. 3D businesses spell these out and get 'buy in' to those behaviours at every level. It's not just about putting 'motivational posters' up highlighting your 'values', it's about making those values meaningful to people in their day to day jobs and there are real tangible benefits in doing so. According to the report *Revealing Key Practices for Effective Recognition*" by management expert Derek Irvine 79 % of employees say recognition tied to core values gave them a stronger sense of company goals and objectives.

This is a simple model that one of our clients uses to encourage the behaviours that they want from their people. They evaluate people on whether they achieve their goals and targets and whether they act in line with the core values and behaviours. For example, people who achieve their targets but don't act in line with the 'preferred behaviours' are 'challenged'. In other words, it's not just about the targets.

Acts In Line With
Preferred Behaviours

'Supported & Encouraged - Sometimes Rewarded	'Championed' Rewarded & Recognised

Doesn't Achieve Objectives ———————————————— Achieves Objectives

'Redirected!'	'Challenged' & Not Rewarded

Doesn't Act In Line With
Preferred Behaviours

'Champion Their Champions'. They encourage, acknowledge, support and Reward those that promote and act in line with the 'core values' as well as their goals and targets. Equally, they...

'Challenge Their Challengers'. They deal with those individuals who do not. What happens in your organisation to those who don't? If the answer is nothing, then expect some people to take the 'easy option' of not bothering.

Virgin boss Sir Richard Branson spoke at the Society For Human Resource Management Conference in 2013 about the importance of creating and sustaining a culture that differentiates a business and anyone who doesn't act in line with that culture, and particularly any leaders who don't reinforce it, should be 'challenged'. He was quoted as saying *"A bad CEO or Manager can destroy the whole spirit of a company incredibly quickly. HR needs to push them out the door."*

How good is your business at Recognising your star performers and spotting people doing things well? Why not get your customers to do it?

A friend who's a regular flyer with American Airlines received some $50 vouchers to use. Not to give him discounts, or extra services, but to give to members of American Airlines staff who made his trip an enjoyable one.

What a great idea - a direct **R**eward for excellent customer service. It happened to us at a hotel we stayed at some years ago. We were given a token that we had to give to the person who made our stay a great one. Apparently the staff could then trade in the rewards for prizes.

It's clear that in lots of businesses, 'recognition' doesn't simply happen. A report from One4all Rewards reveals that business leaders who say 'Thank you' have more motivated staff, higher rates of staff retention, find it easier to recruit and have better reputations. It might seem very obvious stuff, but it's clear that there are lots of business leaders who still don't get it.

The report highlights that 20% of employees say they never receive any form of thanks from their employer and 75% of workers feel that they don't receive sufficient gratitude from their boss for the work that they do.

However, do be careful how you reward your people as a result.

3D 'UnDemonstrated': Getting the Rewards Wrong

One shop Andy visited once asked customers to nominate 'employees of the month'. He came across one, a seventeen year old lad called Brett who gave exceptional service. Andy told him he was going to vote for him. *'Please don't'* he said, 'I've already had 4 nominations this week'. *'You'll win, then'* Andy told him. *'I know'* he replied *'I don't want to… the prize is you get to go for dinner with the MD!'*

THINK IN 3D... THE 7 CHARACTERISTICS OF 'DRAMATICALLY AND DEMONSTRABLY DIFFERENT' BUSINESSES

3D Businesses make sure their 'Rewards' are ones that their people want!

Consider 'Systemising' It. No, this doesn't mean that you HAVE to have an 'employee of the month' award. It's about having some form of process that helps you identify those who are doing these 'good' things. This process could involve your leaders, your staff and even your customers.

So, when it comes to recognising and rewarding your people...
- **What 'behaviours' do you want from your people?**
- **Do they know that?**
- **Do you?**
- **Do you reward and recognise the 'behaviours' that you want from your people?**
- **Do those rewards work?**

5 Questions To Ask Yourself (...And Others.)

Creating the culture you want is not an overnight job and it's certainly not a 'paper exercise', but here are 5 questions to get you thinking, and hopefully get you to actually do something.

Question 1: What's Our Current 'Culture'?
One delegate at a conference Andy spoke at on the subject came up to him after and explained although he found what we talked about on culture fascinating, he was troubled. *"We don't have a culture at our place,"* he explained. *"You do,"* Andy replied. *"We don't,"* he assured him. Andy suggested that if he spent only a few minutes in his offices, he'd get a feel for it relatively quickly. *"We definitely don't have a culture,"* he persisted, *"no one gives a damn at our place." "THAT'S your culture!"* Andy cried.

So, getting a clear 'objective' view of your current culture is a useful point to start from. Why not get your people to describe it – pluses and minuses. Which aspects are they happy with? Which are they unhappy with? Getting a true picture helps you work out what you need to keep, eliminate and work on. Think baby and bathwater.

Question 2: How Do We Want It To Be?
Is there a consistency in approach? Is it spelt out? Getting 'ownership' is key. It should not just be seen as a 'management thing'.

Question 3: What Do We Value?
What do people get 'rewarded' and 'recognised' for in

your business? Are they the things that help create the culture that we want?

Question 4: Do Our Systems and Processes Help Or Hinder?

Your systems and processes do one of two things: they support and reinforce your 'preferred' behaviours or they suppress and detract from them. What's happening in your business?

Question 5: What Are Our Leaders Like As Role Models?

This is all about what your people think. Are your leaders doing the right things, not just saying them? Are they 'visible?'

Some Final Thoughts On Culture...

Culture is 'the way we do things around here', and in **3D** Businesses this does not happen by chance. It is managed, it is embedded and it is lead.

As you've hopefully seen, your culture is shaped by...

your working environment... your organisational 'history'... your customers and marketplace... your people... your systems and processes... your policies and procedures... your 'war stories'... your goals and targets... your rewards and recognitions... your signs and symbols... your customs and rituals... and your leadership (plus lots more.)

All these things do it ...
Positively or... negatively
Deliberately or... accidentally
Consciously or... unconsciously
Your challenge is to work out what's happening in your business...

And then establish...

What needs to happen

So before we move on to #Characteristic 6... Let's take a minute to reflect on #Characteristic 5:

- **What is your 'culture' – the good, the bad and the ugly?**

- **What do you want and need it to be?**

- **What needs to happen to make it UBER?**

"You're going to have a culture anyway. You can and should influence it – so why not build the one you love?"

Dharmesh Shah, the co-founder of of HubSpot.

9. 3D Characteristic # 6: <u>KeeP</u> In Control.

The 7 'Characteristics' of 3D Businesses are:

#1: Get That Vision Thing!

#2: Think in **3D**!

#3: Create Delighted and Devoted Customers

#4: Forget CRM – Think MCR:
'*Maximise* Customer Relationships'

#5: Create an UBER Culture

#6: KeeP In Control

#7: InnovatiON!

This chapter will look at how you

#<u>K</u>ee<u>P</u> In Control

"Not everything that can be counted counts, and not everything that counts can be counted"

Albert Einstein

THINK IN 3D... THE 7 CHARACTERISTICS OF 'DRAMATICALLY AND DEMONSTRABLY DIFFERENT' BUSINESSES

When It Comes To <u>Kee</u><u>P</u>ing <u>I</u>n Control Here Are 10 Things We See 3D Businesses Doing

They…

1. Know what counts...
They understand the key drivers for success of their business in the areas that count.

2. Measure it…
They develop their own 'recipe' of 'key drivers' and that's what they measure.

3. Establish KPI's…
They establish a set of Key Performance Indicators that tell them how they are doing in those areas

4. Systemise it...
They establish simple systems to ensure that the relevant information is collected, analysed and communicated, in a meaningful and timely way.

5. Maximise information…
They recognise that information is good, but it's what they do with it that counts. They ensure that people who need it, get the information they need, when they need it, and in a format they understand.

6. See the bigger picture...
As well as 'on the spot' information, they create 'pictures' and trends to allow them to see the bigger picture and to think 'strategically' ON the business.

7. Have a real profit focus...
They have a clear 'profit focus' with everyone understanding what profit is, where it comes from, and how it can be improved.

8. Create ownership...
They also ensure that everyone in the business has a clear understanding of the impact of what they do (and don't do) has on profitability.

9. Establish clear 'routes' to profitability...
They establish clear profit targets and get 'buy in' to the agreed plans to achieve those profits. It's not about spreadsheets and financial trickery, but it's about taking a proactive approach to maximise financial returns.

10. Maintain 'the balance'...
As well as focusing on the financials, this is not at the cost of sufficient 'delighted and devoted customers' and 'committed, motivated and effective people – they recognise and maximise the links between the three.

It's All About Your Dashboard

If **3D** Characteristic #1 'Get That Vision Thing' is your destination, then Characteristic #6 KeeP In control is the 'dashboard' in your car. In the same way as your dashboard has key indicators that tell you whether you've got any petrol left, your engine's temperature and the oil pressure, **3D** Businesses have indicators that tell them their key indicators: things like sales figures, profit margins, customer satisfaction levels. The best ones have the equivalent of 'sat nav' that use the information to predict whether they're on time, on budget, and that they're actually getting there.

We come across many businesses that are being driven without that dashboard. (To be honest, we come across many who don't have the destination either – they don't have 'that vision thing'.)

What do you measure in your business? What do you record and analyse? Do these things *really* drive performance? Are your 'measures' really helping you focus your time, efforts and resources, in the areas that count?

3D Businesses recognise that information is good, but it's what you do with it that counts. They ensure that the people who need it, get the information they need, when they need it, and in a format they understand and it starts at the top.

This means that they create a set of measures that help them 'KeeP In control' and maximise the performance of their business.

The Benefits Of <u>Kee</u><u>P</u>ing <u>I</u>n Control

3D Businesses tell us that the benefits include:
It...

- **Helps see the 'bigger picture' (we're back to thinking strategically 'ON' the business)**
- **Keeps them on track**
- **Creates focus...on the things that count and at every level of the business**
- **Helps spot trends – good and bad**
- **Helps anticipate problems and identify opportunities**
- **Develops common understanding of what's important**
- **Establishes ownership and accountability**
- **Allows them to celebrate 'successes'**

And very importantly...

- **Helps them sleep in their beds at night!**

Some key questions for your business..

- **Do you have the information you need to drive your business forward?**
- **Does it come to you in a timely useable way?**
- **Do you actually use it?**
- **Do you share it?**

The Common Barriers To Kee<u>P</u>ing <u>I</u>n Control

Unfortunately, lots of businesses struggle with it.

Some of the common barriers to making it all work include:

- **They focus on the wrong stuff...**
  They don't actually work out what's important to the performance of their business and as a result they measure the wrong things.

- **It's 'just about the money'...**
  They make the mistake of only looking at the financial performance of the business (often influenced by bank managers and accountants).

- **It's historical (or 'hysterical'!)...**
  They have incredibly accurate information, but it's out of date and not much use in this fast moving world we're in.

- **It's all about the chase...**
  The senior people chase the information they need as and when they need it – often depending on their mood, time and priorities (of the day). As a result, people wait to be asked and then provide it, rather than supplying the relevant information in a proactive and timely manner.

- **There's no 'ownership' or 'consequences'...**
  A quote we like and use in our seminars is 'What gets measured, gets managed'. We recently

came across this quote from Frederick Reicheld of Net Promoter Score fame. He says "What gets measured creates accountability". Too many businesses simply don't create that accountability.

- **It's all just vanity…**
  Facebook 'likes', number of Twitter followers, and page views, can all be useful indicators for some businesses, but they are not necessarily the 'be all' as some say. Of course, 'likes' and 'followers' are nice, but who's 'following' you and 'liking' you? Are the 'metrics' you're using a key driver of performance for your business or just making you feel good?

- **Drowning in data...**
  The 'key' issue when it comes to Key Performance Indicators is 'Key'. Unfortunately, too many businesses try to measure anything and everything – there are simply too many KPI's. **3D** Businesses recognise it's about creating focus.

- **They don't get used...**
  This when you go to all the effort to collect the information, analyse it, and even publicise it, but do nothing with it.

- **'Big Brother'...**
  This is when the measurement of things creates a 'fear factor' - people think they are being 'spied on'. Very often it's because that the 'why's and wherefores' haven't been explained (in a way that means something to people.)

- **The 'big stick'...**
  The result of this can be people behaving to fulfil the KPI measurement rather than what's right for the business.

3D 'UnDemonstrated': You're Measuring The Wrong Thing...

A client we were working with proudly told us that his people always answered the phone in 3 rings and that this was monitored and measured regularly. We did a number of calls to his business and had to report back that yes, his people did consistently answer the calls in less than 3 rings, but all they were doing was giving poor customer service quicker. (Of course, we're not saying that answering the phone in 3 rings isn't important, but if that's all that's measured, there can be problems.

---

3 Questions for your business:

- What are your 'barriers'?
- How can you remove them?
- It's not you is it?

Making It Work For You

3D Demonstrated: Webmart...

Webmart have a clear set of key performance indicators that are widely published for all to see – they appear on electronic screens all over their offices as numbers, as figures and as graphs and images. It's a clear message as to what is important. Many of the KPI's are 'traditional' measures and focus on sales, profits, margins, enquiries and customer satisfaction.

An interesting KPI that they have is 'Employment Happiness' and all employees on leaving the building for the day are asked to 'Rate Their Day' on a touch screen. Again, the ratings are available for all to see. MD Simon Biltcliffe believes that there's a direct correlation between 'morale' and performance, and as a result he measures it.

So, how can you make this work in your business?

It might not be about measuring 'happiness' just yet, but it's completely up to you.

Here's a simple framework...

1. Establish Your 'Key Drivers'.
There is a clear differentiation between 3D Businesses and the others. While the others focus measuring things right, successful ones focus on measuring the right things. They ask 'what information do we need to

maximise our performance?' and work backwards from
there. The challenge is to ensure that the appropriate
things are measured.

It might seem simple, but start by working out what's
'Key'.
- What information do you need to maximise your
performance?
- What does your 'vision' call for?
- How will you know that your 'Dramatic Difference' is
delivering?

It's typically a balance that reflects your vision, your
goals and targets, operational performance, customer
satisfaction, employee effectiveness and motivation. In
fact our original 'triangle model' is a good starting point:
Do your information systems provide you with relevant,
up to date measures on:

Creating sufficient delighted and devoted customers
e.g. customer satisfaction levels, repeat business, sales
and marketing effectiveness.

**Developing committed, motivated and effective
people** e.g. morale, motivation levels, staff turnover
levels, ideas generated, training outcomes, operational
performance targets.

Maximising financial returns e.g. sales targets, profit/
loss, debtors, creditors, cash-flow, margins.

3D Demonstrated: The Desert Island Question...

The MD of a successful fast growing software development business explained to us that for many years he struggled to think and work 'strategically' and regularly got bogged down in the 'day to day'. It was holding his business back.

A 'spark' for him came on one of our business development programmes. He recognised that a key issue was that he spent far too much time 'at the sharp end', asking lots of questions and chasing information that his people should have been providing him systematically. Typically, he'd 'drop in' on one of his team's offices one morning and ask lots of questions about their sales figures, customer satisfaction levels, progress against production and development performance.

It was different questions each time, based on the different 'issues' of the week, or what he'd suddenly thought of at 2.00am that morning. Sure enough, most times they came up with the answers and all the facts and figures and off he'd go to the next department. He recognised that, human behaviour being what it is, although his people had the answers, they were simply waiting for him to drop by and ask.

So, he decided to take a more strategic approach and sat down and thought *"If I was away on a desert island and could only ring up each team once a week for five minutes, what would I want to know?"* It was a 'light bulb moment' for him – he then sat down with each departmental head and discussed what he wanted from them, in what format and when. They then established some simple formal reporting mechanisms to ensure he got the information he needed, when he wanted it, and in the format that worked for him. Surprise, surprise, it allowed him to concentrate on his 'proper job', created accountability in each department and eliminated the 'upward delegation' he had been encouraging.

If you were on a desert island, and could only make a five minute call...

what would you want (and need) to know?

 THINK IN 3D... THE 7 CHARACTERISTICS OF 'DRAMATICALLY AND DEMONSTRABLY DIFFERENT' BUSINESSES

2. Establish KPI's

Once you've established what your key drivers are, you need to identify how you'll measure them. Your challenge is to identify which indicators are right for your business. (Remember, focus on quality of information, rather than quantity. You can always increase the number of KPI's once your systems are established).

Ensure they are 'measurable' and specific. For example...

'Customer satisfaction levels' might be: '% of customers who are 'completely happy' with us this month / this year' (by department, by office).

Marketing activity might be: Number of enquiries received this week, number and value of quotes done this week, number of orders won this week.

Notice that they are 'specific', 'measurable', and have a time frame allocated to them.

3D Demonstrated: From 'Financials' To 'Focus'...

The managing partner of a growing law firm with 6 different departments had basic financial controls which were managed 'en masse' by the practice manager. He produced monthly reports and graphs showing the firm's total monthly results, but they were nearly all focused just on the financials, and everything was 'grouped together' for the firm as a whole.

The managing partner and her team recognised that the keys to their ongoing success were the obvious...

- Achieving fee earning and profitability targets in every department
- Individual fee earners hitting their fee earning targets

But the key drivers for success for them were..
- Creating new clients from networking and profile raising activity
- Getting existing clients to spend more – there was very little (if any 'cross-selling')
- Clients making recommendations to others

Yet, there was no measure of any of these things. So, as well as their monthly 'financials', they established their monthly KPI's for each department as...
- Achievement of financial targets (broken down by individual fee earners)
- Gross margin total
- Number of new opportunities (created by which sources)
- Number of new clients (created by which sources)
- Client satisfaction levels based on NPS (see later in this chapter)
- Amount of business created as repeat business
- Amount of business created as a cross – sell from another department (and which department it was)
- Amount of business created as a referral.

Departmental measurements improved overall accountability and performance rapidly, as well as effectiveness and focus of partner and departmental meetings, and company communication.

The result? A more focused and profitable business.

3. Maximise the information

In **3D** Businesses the relevant information is collected, analysed, communicated and maximised.

3D	Typical occurrences in Non 3D Businesses
Collected	Relevant information not collected / the wrong information collected
Analysed	Relevant information not being analysed / being analysed and ignored
Communicated	Information never reaching the appropriate people / arriving too late / in a format that cannot be understood / or being hidden amongst irrelevant information
Maximised	People doing nothing with the information.

3D Businesses reverse this model. They start with the 'Maximised' – what do we need? (It's the 'Desert Island' question) and then work out how they are going to get it. They establish and agree responsibility, frequency and nature of collection, analysis of data and information. They create templates; tools and guidelines for collecting and analysing it. They also establish systems for communicating and sharing it, and the important bit – they create accountability and timeframes for doing so.

A key factor of success in maximising information is plotting 'trends' and seeing the bigger picture. It's about building a cumulative view of what's happening – are the gaps month-on-month getting bigger or smaller – and what needs to be done?

4. Share the information... in a way that works.

Do you ever feel that in today's fast moving business world, you're constantly bombarded with information and sometimes it's difficult to take it all in? Well your people may well be thinking that too.

Have you ever shared information that's important and relevant to those that you are sharing it with, but somehow it doesn't seem to get through? The data is there, but it's just not hitting the spot.

3D Businesses keep their people informed about progress in terms of financial and non-financial information, and they do so in an easy to understand format. They recognise that most of us don't understand balance sheets, liquidity ratios, and all that stuff.

So they establish systems to transfer it around and through the business in a timely and meaningful way ('timely and meaningful' as defined by the recipients, not the sender). Our experience suggests graphs and pictures work better than figures.

For example, many of us prefer to visualise things rather than just see 'numbers' – we like to see things in 'pictures'. If you're anything like us, we're sure that may well have been influenced by the eager anticipation each week of the Blue Peter Appeal 'Totaliser' when we were kids!

3D Demonstrated: Ella's Kitchen

We mentioned Ella's Kitchen huge transparent glass tube in their reception that is very visible to all to see. It has markings up its side representing sales targets for the business with their 'vision' target of a billion 'tiny tummy touch – points' at the top.

Every quarter, the team drop in the appropriate number of cartons of their products that represent their sales that quarter as they aim to fill it towards the top. It's a very public, symbolic thing, and everyone in the business understands how well they're doing on the journey to that one billion.

Effective information flow is a key factor in 'engaging people' and in maximising performance at an operational level. The key is communicating the information to individuals to allow them to do that.

Things we've seen work well...
- Plot trends, not just isolated figures
- Use graphs, symbols, pictures, etc, not just figures
- Consider 'Traffic Light' systems. (Green is fine; amber is a warning; red means there's a problem)
- Don't bombard people with information – work out what is 'key'
- Encourage questions/comments about the results
- Put formal time aside to deal with them
- Celebrate successes
- Ensure people understand the consequences of positive and negative results.

3D Demonstrated: Excellent Customer Service? You've Had Your Chips!

Here's a great example of a business that measures customer satisfaction in a very imaginative, visible and effective way. Diners at The Bull's Head in Repton, Derbyshire are given two roulette chips – a green one with "Food" on it and a brown one with "Service" on it. Diners are asked to place the chips in one of five boxes numbered one for 'poor' through to five for 'excellent'. These chips represent what customers thought about the food and the service.

The chips are collected each day and the results graphs are available for all staff to see. Staff are rewarded for the 'excellence' levels – if the 'excellence' levels hit 70%, staff get a £10 voucher, 80%, it's £20 and 90% it's £50 in cash. In the British Institute Of Innkeepers magazine, Richard and Loren Pope who run the pub, explained that they only focus on the 'excellents' as it's those customers who are four times more likely to return than others.

It's a nice example of a) getting and keeping 'customer service' on the agenda b) rewarding consistently great performance, and c) 'Demonstrating' (to both customers and staff what's important and how they're doing.

Some businesses are very transparent with their KPIs.

3D Demonstrated: Resolve IT Solutions Show Everyone What Customers Think

Resolve IT Solutions are great at customer service (we know because we're customers – and no, we haven't been 'incentivised' to say this). They are a forward thinking Sheffield based IT supplier who have come up with a 'Dramatically Different' way of 'Demonstrating' their excellence in this area. They publicise ALL their customer feedback 'live' on their website. It's a brave move.

Every time the Resolve team fix a customer's problem, they send them an e-mail to let them know, and ask them to click on one of 3 smileys – "Excellent", "Satisfactory" and "Not So Good". They also ask how well they responded to and fixed issues within their agreed timescales (currently at an impressive 98%).

Some (who don't know them) might say 'anyone can make these up', and yes they can. However, having 'experienced' it as a customer, most people see it as a Demonstration that their experience was not a 'one off'.

Think information to empower, not as power. Here's a great question to ask your team. *"What information do you need to do your job better?"* Follow it up with - *"How will this help?"*

Then, consider establishing systems that give it to them (in a format they can understand). If you want people to make management decisions, it's vital you give them management information.

Just One Question...

How do you know if all this **3D thinking** is paying off? **3D** Businesses measure whether they're doing it right – and many use just one direct question to do it.

That one direct question is:

"On a scale of 0 to 10, how likely is it that you would recommend us to a friend or colleague?"

It's a simple question that is the basis of the internationally recognised Net Promoter Score (NPS) Many **3D** Businesses measure the loyalty of their customers with the Net Promoter Score which is a great simple tool that was developed by Fred Reichheld, Bain & Company, and Satmetrix back in 2003. It's an approach that has been adopted by lots of forward thinking businesses including; E.ON, Philips, GE, Apple Retail, American Express, First Direct, and Intuit.

Those that rate you 9 or 10 (out of 10) are your Active Promoters (people who rave about you.) Those that score you 7 or 8 are your 'Passives' – they like you but don't shout about it. Those that rate you 0-6 are your 'Detractors' (the ones who aren't so keen). Your Net Promoter Score (NPS) is the % of Active Promoters – % of Detractors.

It's powerful because it doesn't take into account the 7's and 8's (the 'Passives' – those who think you're ok) and can be (and should be) used to measure whether all this stuff is working.

It's worth pointing out that a 'follow up' question 'why / why not'? can be a useful way of creating 'dialogue' and helping you develop understanding too.

That's all very well, but does it actually mean anything? Well, there's some evidence from Bruce Temkin of Customer Experience Matters that it certainly does. His organisation examined NPS scores for companies across 19 industries based on feedback from 10,000 U.S. consumers, and more than 95,000 pieces of feedback from consumers about those companies. His research found that:

- **Promoters are almost six times as likely to forgive.** They asked consumers about their likelihood to forgive a company if it delivered a bad experience and found that **64% of promoters** are likely to forgive compared with **11% of detractors.**
- **Promoters are more than five times as likely to repurchase. 81% of promoters** are likely to repurchase additional products and service compared with **16% of detractors.**
- **Promoters are more than twice as likely as detractors to actually recommend. 64% of promoters** have recommended the company compared with **24% of detractors.**

You can obviously plot your ongoing score, score by office or department, even individual account handler! You can also use it to benchmark your business against others and to measure improvements in performance. In the UK, Apple have an NPS of 67, First Direct has a NPS of 61 (and, if you're interested, Andy Hanselman Consulting has an **NPS** of 64).

So, if you're only going to ask one question, then **"On a scale of 0 to 10, how likely is it that you would recommend us to a friend or colleague?"** might be a good start?.

Don't just limit it to customers though. More and more businesses are using to measure their employee's 'satisfaction' at work – how would your team score it?

Dare you find out?

Create A Profit Focus...

20 odd years ago when we had just set up in business, a friend of Andy's who'd always worked for someone else asked if he was up for going away for a weekend. Andy explained that he couldn't really afford it as money was tight. Indignantly, he replied *'No money? That's ridiculous. You run your own company – give yourself a pay rise.'*

Most people don't know how business works. It's not their fault – nobody teaches them.

Many think that profit is what goes in your back pocket. In fact, some think that ALL your sales revenue goes in your back pocket. Others make calculations in their mind like this. *"We charge £100 per hour and I get paid £10 per hour - that means they make £90 an hour for each of us - no wonder he drives a BMW."*

It's not their fault. Nobody gets taught this stuff at school. They don't get it explained at college and most don't get taken through it at work. Many companies don't share any sort of financial information with their staff, but expect them to take responsibility for profitability. Others do share it, but do so in a way that people don't understand – lots of figures, tables and calculations. It might as well be in Japanese.

Those that don't share any information at all often have a naive belief that their people aren't interested, or even worse, because they'll worry if things aren't too good, it's best not to let them know. In our experience, most people can tell if things are bad; deliveries aren't going through the door, orders aren't coming in, and suppliers aren't being paid – their biggest concern is that 'the management' haven't noticed it and aren't doing anything about it.

3D Businesses create a profit focus and ensure that people understand how they can impact on profitability, both positively and negatively. Their leaders provide people with meaningful information to help them maximise their own performance and that of the company.

So, involve and educate your people about how business works and share with them relevant and understandable financial information. This allows you to get them to understand how much it costs to run the business, the value of their own contribution, and how much things cost. It also helps you to encourage ideas to save money, reduce waste and increase profits.

3D Demonstrated: 'Mine's A Pint'...

A pub landlord shows his new employees a pint glass and half fills it with beer "That's the brewery's share" he explains. He fills it 3/4's full "That's for Customs and Excise". He then tops it up to just below the top "This goes to running the pub and paying your wages" and finally as the last few drops top the glass up, he says "And this is the profit that allows us to develop the business".

By the way, we suggest that 'educating' employees and getting them to understand finance and profitability is not simply left to the accountants. Often they're too 'in love' with financial terminology, spreadsheets and complex ratios. Sorry, that's a generalisation, and if you can get them to explain stuff without these, then let them loose. If not, keep them well away.

3D Demonstrated: 'The Price Is Right'...

'The Price Is Right' is a great interactive exercise we run in client businesses that gets people to guess how much the business spends on different things in a year. It's a useful way of introducing the basic running costs of the business in a 'fun', educational, and non-threatening way. We breakdown the total costs of running the business in a year into 'headings' (e.g. people costs, rent, rates and building costs) and then get them to work in teams to guess how much they spend on each element. We then show them the actual amounts. They have to then see how far they were 'out', and whichever team was 'out' the least gets a prize.

You'll be amazed at how surprised they are (most have honestly never thought about it before). It's also a subtle way of letting people know just how much work is needed to cover costs, run the business, and even make some profit.

3D Businesses find ways of explaining the financial make-up of their business in simple terms. How many products do they need to sell a day/a week just to open the doors and to cover their costs? How many deliveries do they need to make? How many customers need to book their services? How many hours a week do they need to 'charge out' to customers to break even every month?

An 'educated' and 'empowered' team are far more likely to generate profit improvement ideas. Find ways to get people to identify profit improvement ideas. Give them time to do it. It has to be 'blame free' and constructive. Consider rewarding the best (or all) of the ideas – base it on cost savings or profit improvement.

Getting people to understand the profit implications of their improvement ideas and suggestions helps them put a value on their contributions. It also allows you to do the same.

Establish Your Route To Profitability...

3D Businesses create 'A Route To Profitability'. Hopefully your 'vision' has some reference to profit targets, or if you're in a non-profit making business (deliberately non-profit making that is) to 'maximising financial returns'.

That means you need a profit improvement plan which is all about exploring all the options your business has to do that.

Have a look at this model that explores the options you have, hopefully you'll recognise that they are basically a culmination of lots of the things we've been exploring in this book.

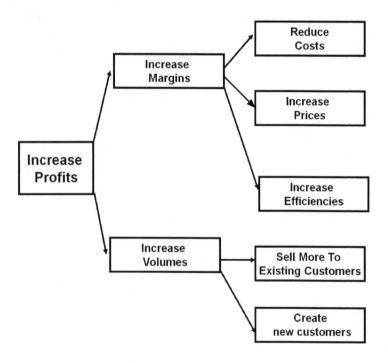

The basic options that your business has to maximise profitability are:

Option 1: Reduce Costs...

This means reducing your overheads or running costs. In today's very competitive marketplaces, most businesses already run a tight ship, and therefore the opportunities to significantly reduce overheads may be limited. However, that doesn't mean you shouldn't look closer at your overheads. Start with your major costs, and then move through the others. (Warning! Don't spend vast amounts of time and effort 'penny pinching' for small gains. If you're not careful it ends up costing you more than you save). Talk to your suppliers. Find out how they could add value to your business. Again, review your major costs - are you getting the best value? Can you negotiate better deals? What would you need to offer in return? Remember, cheapest isn't always best.

Option 2: Increase Prices...

Put your prices up. Or maybe put some of your prices up. Establish a pricing policy, set targets. If it's difficult to get prices up with existing customers, establish a new pricing regime for future work. Think about your options - What more do you need to do/offer to get prices up, and increase your margins? Think about low cost (to you) extras, additional support, advice and help that add to your Dramatic Difference that cost effectively increase the overall value of what customers receive. Be imaginative with your pricing - adjust for seasonality, availability, time, date, type of customer. Be adventurous, and be brave. You know you're worth it!

Also, find out if there are things that you provide that customers don't really value – create that dialogue. If they are not adding value, then they are adding cost – consider reducing or getting rid of them.

Option 3: Increase Efficiency...

This means increasing the speed at which you turn, for example, £1.00 into £1.50. Look at your production methods; Are there opportunities to improve? Could technology help? Do your people have any ideas? Get them involved, generate solutions, and improvements.

Can certain tasks be done by someone who earns less? For example, accountants, lawyers and others in professional services often use junior, or less experienced people to carry out certain tasks (whilst maintaining the quality of work, of course). This might even mean 'outsourcing' things. Yes, it costs, but if it frees people up to maximise more profitable work, it might be worth considering. Look at your own role - how much time do you spend being an overpaid administrator? Significant gains can be made by getting more efficient and effective at what you do as a business. The impacts on profitability tend to be longer lasting. Keep working at it. Imagine the power of a business that gets better every day.

Identify your key generators of errors, waste and complaints, educate your people, inspire (and reward) them to eliminate the causes of errors and waste – engage them (it's that UBER Culture thing again!).

Option 4: Sell More To Your Existing Customers...

This is all about Maximising your Customer Relationships – of course, avoid 'bombarding' customers with 'junk mail', but target your offers. Develop a pro-active programme of education. Get closer to your customers, find out what they think, want and need. Establish the % of customer share with key customers and identify opportunities to sell on. Be imaginative - find 'excuses' to talk to and visit customers. Keep in touch, (get back in touch) add value, develop relationships. If you've got different departments, establish ways to encourage and increase 'cross selling'. Discover what other products/services your customers are purchasing - is that an opportunity for you? What do customers want? What would they pay more for? Start with your existing customers. Can you 'leverage' your relationships? Who else in their organisation might have a need for your products/services? Generate referrals. How? Ask for them. Develop a proactive approach to creating referrals. Reward and incentivise your current customers.

Option 5: Create More Customers...

Start by looking at your 'best' customers. Why do they buy from you? What's important to them? How can you find more like them? It's important to establish a business generating system to create leads and new customers. Proactivity and targeting are the key. Do not just sit back and wait for the business to come in. The chances are, it won't. Establish which new markets make sense for you. Stick as close to your core market as possible, initially, and work outwards. Do your research. Allow time. Develop a plan and set targets. Again, set up a proactive lead generation process and stick to it. Don't take your eye off the ball from your current customers.

Your challenge is to explore all the options and create a recipe for your business. Tip: involve others, get their ideas and input to...

Create A Route To Profitability For Your Business.

So before we move on to our last #Characteristic 7…
Let's take a minute to reflect on #Characteristic 6:

- **What are the key drivers for your business?**

- **What information do you need to help maximise your performance?**

- **What needs to happen to help you KeeP In Control?**

"A business without a path to profitability is just a hobby"

Jason Fried & David Heinemeier Hansson, 37 Signals

10. 3D Characteristic # 7: InnovatiON!

The 7 'Characteristics' of 3D Businesses are:

#1: Get That Vision Thing!

#2: Think in **3D**!

#3: Create Delighted and Devoted Customers

#4: Forget CRM – Think MCR:
   '*Maximise* Customer Relationships'

#5: Create an UBER Culture

#6: KeeP In Control

#7: InnovatiON!

This chapter will look at how you make

#InnovatiON work for you

"If you do something and it turns out pretty good, then you should go do something else wonderful, not dwell on it for too long. Just figure out what's next"

Sir Jonathan Ive, Apple

When It Comes To InnovatiON! here Are 10 Things We See 3D Businesses Doing.

They…

1. Understand what it is and isn't...
They know it's not necessarily lots of revolutionary new products and services, hours of 'blue sky thinking', but proactively sourcing, generating and implementing new ideas

2. Put it on the agenda...
They ensure it's an integral part of what they do and supports and enhances their 'Dramatic Difference'

3. Are proactive...
They proactively work ON identifying and seeking ways that InnovatiON can contribute to helping them achieve their vision and in the 'areas that count'

4. Ensure their leaders act as role models...
Their leaders drive this at every level of the business. They encourage and support their people to do the same

5. Build systems and process...
They establish simple processes to generate ideas and suggestions from customers, their people and their support networks

6. Create the climate...
They engage everyone to get involved and contribute, and create a supportive culture that encourages, allows and supports people to do so

7. Challenge the status quo...
They allow, encourage, even push people to constructively question and 'challenge the status quo', what they do, and how they do it

8. Create time...
They help their people create time to get out of the 'day to day', out of their own teams and departments and their 'comfort zones'

9. Support...
Time, effort and resources are put into making things happen and this is monitored and measured – it is certainly not left to chance

10. Take action not notes...
Implementation is all about 'making it happen' and doing something with the ideas generated.

So What Exactly is Innovation?

The definition of innovation that we use is…

'The successful exploitation of new ideas'

and in **3D** Businesses it's a way of life.

By definition that means for them it's all about….
* Finding or creating new ideas…
* Doing something with them…..
* And measuring the impacts

And doing this consistently and continuously!

The key bit is 'the exploitation' or as consultants Booze & Co call it 'conversion'. Their report on the world's most innovative businesses stated that; *"Our report shows that organisations that were effective at conversion of ideas had 8% higher revenue growth than those that weren't".*

See? It's all about the 'doing'… a key differentiator in **3D** Businesses

They work hard to overcome the common barriers to innovation – do you recognize any of these in your business?

10 Common Barriers To Maximising Innovation

The common barriers we see are...

1. 'We've always done it like this'... A culture that creates a reluctance and resistance to change and sometimes it's at the top of the business. The *Eyes Wide Shut!: A Report On Innovation In The UK* states that 57% of UK leaders say their management team is failing to lead effectively for innovation (that's over half).

2. No 'processes'... there are no formal processes to seek and generate ideas. The Eyes Wide Shut report says that only 40% of UK's employees are satisfied with the opportunities that exist to feed their views and ideas upwards to senior managers. 'My door is always open' is NOT a process by the way.

3. Fear!... people are scared of putting their head above the parapet and criticism of their ideas and suggestions.

4. It's just about new products and services... there is a view that innovation is solely about coming up with new products or services rather than improving what is done.

5. It's a 'management thing'... and that frontline staff's ideas and opinions don't count!

6. No 'rewards'... A report by ORC International suggests that less than half of respondents feel that innovation and creativity are highly valued in their workplace, and employees in the UK are less likely to feel that they would be recognised for coming up with new and innovative ways of working. In other words, there's no 'incentive' to make it happen.... even worse, the reward is 'more work'!

7. What's the BIG idea?... The focus is on the 'next big thing' rather than lots of, or even just one, small one.

8. Silos.... people do not interact or engage with other teams or departments – either through 'habit', or worse, they are 'not allowed'. Back to the Eyes Wide Shut Report, 59% of UK leaders say bureaucracy stops innovative ideas before they reach fruition and this is exasperated by silos.

9. Insufficient (no?) time allocated or allowed.... individuals are not encouraged to create specific time for 'innovation'. 58% of UK leaders believe their teams have no problem coming up with ideas, but 62% say it is almost impossible to gain support to test and develop them.

10. It's not on the agenda.... 53% of UK leaders believe they are missing out on innovation opportunities because employees cannot see the bigger picture. Again, this is about a lack of 'strategic thinking' and consciously looking ahead at opportunities and threats, and encouraging others to do the same.

Do you recognise any of these things in your business? No? Are you sure that you're looking hard enough? So, what's the answer?

Well, employees from businesses from around the world were asked for their opinions on the key elements of organisational innovation in the Kenexa Work Trends Survey:

This is what they said….

- **Freedom to try new things, even if they might not succeed**
- **Actual action on trying new innovations**
- **Support to implement new ideas**
- **Encouragement to innovate and try new things**

This is what **3D** Businesses address and ensure that it's part of their culture.

They…*'successfully exploit new ideas'* – This doesn't mean being incredibly creative and hours and hours of 'blue sky thinking', but a proactive and systematic approach to sourcing and generating new ideas and then doing something with those ideas. **3D** Businesses recognise that this is an ongoing process and create time to work ON this to **Develop** their **'Dramatic Difference'!**

It's All About Leadership

"Disruptive innovation is not a tactic. It's a mindset"
That's a great quote from Richard Branson at the beginning of a video that celebrates Virgin Records' 40th birthday.

It's a record label that started off with being 'disruptive' by signing up a complete unknown called Mike Oldfield over 40 years ago, then the Sex Pistols in the 70's, Culture Club in the 80's and of course 'girl power' with The Spice Girls. We know they might not seem 'disruptive' now, but they caused a bit of a stir when they started back in the 90's. They supported lots of other 'rebels' (as well as some 'traditionalists') over those 40 years and that 'disruptive innovation' came from the top.

3D Businesses ensure that innovatiON is an integral part of the way they do business! They proactively work ON identifying and seeking ways that innovatiON can contribute to helping them achieve their vision and in the 'areas that count'. Their leaders create time to think and work strategically and get innovatiON on the agenda. They act as role models and drive this at every level of the business. They encourage and support their people to do the same.

What can you do about it? Well a 'starter for 10' is to put 'innovation' on the 'agenda' in your business. Define and explain what it means for your business and encourage others to do the same.

Maybe you could set goals and targets for it. Think about your :
- 'Dramatic Difference' and customer offer
- People's commitment, motivation and effectiveness
- Profitability

As we've seen, so many business leaders get caught up in the 'day to day' tactical stuff that stops them 'thinking strategically and moving things forward. Equally, others get stuck 'up in the clouds' so far away from the 'real world' that they get out of touch with their people and their customers.

The best leaders seem to get the balance right, but how do they do it?

3D Demonstrated: Tim Cook, CEO of Apple

He works hard at it. Here's how...

"Not allowing yourself to become insular is very important—maybe the most important thing, I think, as a CEO." He says on the Church Of The Customer website. He goes on to explain how he consciously 'gets out there' to find out what his people think...

"We want ideas coming from all of our 80,000 people, not five or three. A much smaller number of people have to decide and edit and move forward, but you want ideas coming from everywhere. You want people to explore."

He proactively creates time to find out what his customers think too...

> *"So I'll walk around our stores. You can learn a tremendous amount in a store. I get a lot of e-mails and so forth, but it's a different dimension when you're in a store and talking to customers face to face."*

How much time do you spend 'out there' engaging with the ones that count – namely, your people and your customers - and … do you actually listen to them when you're there?

3 Steps To Get Things Started

Developing an innovation driven business doesn't happen overnight, but it has to start somewhere. The best place is with you. Why not pick one or two of these ideas in this section to get the ball rolling:

1. Ask your people *'What's wrong with our business?'* followed by *"What should we do about it?'*

If you're really brave…. why not ask your customers?

Go on…. we dare you!

2. Spot your 'organisational stupidities
Have you ever spotted something that seems so daft or pointless in someone else's business? You think *'who on earth came up with this idea?'* We call these things 'organisational stupidities'.

There's no real rhyme or reason for them apart from the fact that nobody has either tried to challenge them, or worse, couldn't be bothered to. We've got some bad news for you. They probably exist in your business too. The problem is they're often easier to spot in other businesses than in your own. These typically are the things that you've been doing for years, but don't know why, and nobody seems to challenge or question them. Some very simple examples we've seen…

* **Name badges that just say 'Trainee'**
  What's the point of that? Are we supposed to ignore that particular individual? More importantly, don't they become a real person with a name until they've

served their apprenticeship? (Although it could be worse. A friend once worked part time in the local branch of a major retailer. When Julie arrived on her first day, the manageress informed her she had to wear a name badge at all times. Unfortunately, there wasn't one with Julie on it, so she was told to wear one with Rachel on for the first three weeks!)

- **'Dress Down' Fridays.**
 If dress and attire are so critical in a business every other day what makes it less critical on a Friday? Are customers on that day not as important as those on other days? (PS, We've nothing against a dress code by the way. We just don't understand why one day a month it can be so different - it's a bit like being let out on parole for a day).

- **Meetings without a purpose**
Ask yourself 'what do you want to have achieved at the end of this next two hours?' If you can't answer, call it off. If you find yourself in a meeting someone else has called and that question hasn't been considered, then walk out. Notice we said 'purpose', not 'agenda'. We've been in lots of meetings with agendas, but they were still pointless!

They are just examples – your challenge is to discover and eliminate yours.

3. STOP, START, CONTINUE
A simple, but great way of getting discussion and debate going, and being a role model when it comes to this stuff is to undertake a little exercise we use on our leadership programmes called **STOP, START,**

CONTINUE. Basically, it's about finding out what your people think that you personally should 'Stop, Start, Continue' doing when it comes to leading and managing them. This could be a simple questionnaire (named or anonymously- whatever's best for you and your people) or maybe a group discussion (without you being in the room). Please remember..... the truth sometimes hurts – you have to listen to what's said (One client of ours was told by a team member to 'STOP breathing!').

Establish Systems And Processes

"If you always do what you've always done, you'll always get what you've always had". Although that sounds like something that David Brent from The Office would say, there's a lot of truth in it, particularly if you're talking about improving your competitiveness and getting ahead of your competitors.

The 'finding' of ideas to help differentiate your business is a vital first step, and there are lots of ways of doing this - we all have our own favourites. However, are you guilty of 'always doing the same things' particularly when it comes to spotting, generating and developing ideas?

Are you bombarded with ideas from people in your team? Do they regularly generate suggestions on how your business could improve? Are they forever coming up with new ways of doing things?

Not really? Only sometimes? Never? Is that because that they don't have any ideas? Probably not! It's more likely to be the fact that you don't have any sort of process for them to put forward their ideas.
Research suggests that over a quarter of UK employees (27%) are sitting on ideas that they think would be good for their business but they're not putting those ideas forward. Why? Is it because they're not bothered? No, it's because there's no platform or process for doing so. In fact, the research says that 71% of UK businesses don't have any such platform for contributions to be made.

So, what does a 'platform' look like? Well, it doesn't have to be 'all singing all dancing', but there does need to be some sort of 'process'.

As we highlighted in the 10 common blockages to innovatiON, a key one in many business is that there's **no 'process'.** The problem with 'processes' in lots of business leader's eyes is that it means formality, paperwork, bureaucracy, and rigidity – in fact the opposite can be true, and here's a great example of a **simple innovation 'process'** that could work in any business.

3D Demonstrated: I Wish, I Like, I Wonder...

It comes from Akshay Kothari and Ankit Gupta, two Stanford University students who set up the incredibly successful news gathering 'app'; Pulse, in 2010 and then sold to Linked In for $90 million!

Speaking at one of the Stanford Entrepreneurial Thought Leadership lectures (always well, well worth listening to by the way – on line or via podcast each week), they highlighted a very simple 'process' that they have in their business. On Friday afternoon's the whole team get together for an hour and as well as updating everyone on progress, they all get involved in *'I Like… I Wish. I Wonder...'*

Everyone is encouraged to feed into the team things that they, guess what...
- **'Like'** – things that have gone well, recognition for a job well done, highlighting individual contributions and successes

---

- **'Wish'** – things that need improving, developing and changing
- **'Wonder'** – suggestions, questions, ideas, queries, clarification of things from others (particularly the bosses!)

It's fun, collaborative, engaging and … effective

- **We *like* it!**
- **We *wish* more would do it!**
- **We *wonder* if you will?**

Diarising time into your meetings to do something like this, or even creating a specific time to do this regularly is a 'process'.

3D Businesses establish simple processes to generate ideas and suggestions from customers, their people, and their support networks. Not necessarily lots of sophisticated methods of ideas generation, but practical ways to make it work for them - it could be something as simple as allocating time at a monthly meeting to focus on specific areas of improvement.

They establish processes that work for them and build it into the way they do things.

3D Demonstrated: Simple 'Processes' That Work

Here are a few simple examples we've seen…

Pizza Problem Solving…. The team gets together for an hour over some pizzas at 1.00pm on one

Friday lunchtime a month to generate ideas to overcome a specific business problem or issue (the boss leaves the room to let them get on with it). He comes back in at 1.45 and they put forward their ideas and suggestions. By 2.00pm steps to move things forward are agreed.

Front Line Fix….. Teams are allocated £200 to solve, fix, eliminate or improve a problem system or process that's holding them back, upsetting customers, creating waste, and frustration.

Ten For A Tenner Tuesdays….. A team of individuals are given £10 each to buy a sandwich and a drink at a local café or pub and have a discussion about a specific issue or problem. They are tasked with generating 10 ideas which they bring back to the office and present to the MD (she says she doesn't give them more than a tenner or they don't come back!).

Boss For The Day…. Ask individuals 'If you were the boss here what one thing would you change?' 'Systemise' the process – do it with a different individual each week / month.

Think 'Carlsberg'…… You've seen the adverts. Ask your people 'If Carlsberg ran our business, what would it look like?' Use the ideas to generate discussion.

Creativity and innovation is not prescriptive. What works for one business, won't necessarily work for you, but it *might*. Your challenge is to do something. One idea often leads to another. Hopefully, reading this has ignited a spark. Just do what works for you, or *might* just work for you.

Whatever you do, it's about giving time, permission and encouragement to make this stuff happen. Allow (push?) your people to DO THINGS with the ideas – set a date for 'reporting back', highlight successes and build on the results, 'reward' those who do it – THAT'S a process. Customers can also be a great source of ideas. They can help in two ways;

Firstly, when things go wrong: 'Disappointed' Customers can be a great source of ideas for improvement. As Bill Gates says *"Your most unhappy customers are your greatest source of learning."* The key is of course 'spotting' disappointment and then doing something about it (see Characteristic #3)

Do you have 'formal' systems for getting customer feedback? Maybe you should?

Secondly... get out there! Find out what they think, engage with them, create 'dialogue' and then do something – check out the questions in chapter 8, Characteristic #4: MCR and give your customers a damn good listening to.

A great source of ideas can come from when you solve your customers' problems…

3D Demonstrated: Red Tomato Pizza – Dramatically Different Delivery!

Here's a great way to solve a problem for pizza lovers – worldwide, well Dubai to start with. It's the emergency panic fridge magnet that when pressed automatically orders your favourite pizza to be delivered to your door direct from your local pizza restaurant!!!!

The VIP Pizza Magnet is an innovation from the Red Tomato Pizza company in Dubai. The magnet looks like a little pizza box with a lid that has to be opened before you press the "pull for hunger" button to order your pizza. It's easy to set up, you simply link it to Bluetooth and enter your favourite pizza recipe on the website, along with your address and details, and every time you press the button, a confirmation text is sent and a fresh pizza gets delivered straight to your door.

It's a great example of solving customers 'problems' and creating an opportunity. It certainly seems to have created a 'buzz' when it was launched in Dubai. Word spread so quickly that they ran out of stock of the magnets. New stock was quickly ordered. VIP Magnet is only currently, sadly available in Dubai, but let's hope for a delivery near us soon.

3D Demonstrated: Our Cow Molly

Eddie Andrew thinks in **3D**. As well as providing some of the loveliest ice cream you will ever have (the Our Cow Molly lemon and ginger ice cream is absolutely amazing), he has built a fantastic reputation for his innovative approach in a very 'traditional' industry.

This 'innovative thinking' extends to the most traditional side to the family business - the milk round! His family have delivered milk to folks' door steps directly from their farm for over 60 years and it is currently run by Eddie's brother Dan.

Although things don't always run smoothly in those early mornings, as Eddie explains; *"The way it works is we load the truck up with what we think the customers want / usually have, you walk up their drive and you find there's a note saying they want an extra pint or no milk at all."*

He also knew that customers sometimes go on holiday and forget to let him know or needed an extra pint above their normal delivery.

This got Eddie thinking... the customer has had to find a pen and paper to leave him a note out and he thought 'how old fashioned is that?' So they introduced a texting service that meant that customers could simply let Dan know what they wanted via their mobile phones.

So now their customers text for extra milk. They

don't have to put in their whole address and personal details as Dan has their address stored in his phone. They simply text the amount.

"We only load the truck up with the right amount of milk and we don't have to walk up a drive to find a note saying no milk. Win Win!" explains Eddie.

Why not get some Our Cow Molly ice cream, chill out, and get thinking how you could solve the 'problems' you and your customers have?

Create A Climate For Innovation

Creating and allocating time for innovation is key.
3D Businesses engage everyone to get involved
and contribute, and create a supportive culture that
encourages, allows and supports people to do so. They
allow, encourage, even push people to constructively
question and 'challenge the status quo' and to 'fish
in different ponds' – that means creating time to get
out of the 'day to day', out of their own teams and
departments and their 'comfort zones'. They 'champion
their champions' and reward and recognise those that
get involved and contribute to making innovatiON work
in their business.

So, how do the best 'innovators' do it? According to
some research by Harvard Business School they've
highlighted 5 'secrets' of successful innovators (we're
always nervous about people who promote 'secrets'
– by definition, if you're promoting them, they aren't
'secret' any more, but anyway, here goes)…

They are, apparently (with our interpretations in italics):

Associating – *It's about 'connecting' stuff*
Questioning - *Asking 'why?' 'what if?' ' how?' etc.*
Observing - *Watching others do stuff*
Experimenting – *Trying things out*
Networking – *Meeting and connecting with others*

So, now the secrets are out, what does this mean for
you? Maybe you do some, or all of these things, but do
you always do them in the same environment all the
time?

Do you always attend the same networks, read the same newspapers and magazines, and visit the same websites? Do you always focus on the same businesses when trying to 'get ahead'? If so, maybe you're always getting the same outcomes.

Our recommendation is try 'fishing in different ponds' – that means doing the things above in environments you're not so familiar with. The likelihood then, is that you'll not 'get what you always have'.

3D Leaders don't just 'Think Out Of The Box', they 'Get Out Of The Box'! They 'get out there' and engage with others outside the 'comfort zone' of their own business and area of expertise. From simply creating time to work with other departments and locations across the business, to 'fishing in different ponds' which means other companies, other industries, even other countries and cultures. As well as doing it themselves, they encourage others to do so too.

3D Demonstrated: Create a DIY MBA

It's our friend, the forthright and forward thinking leader of the business Webmart, Simon Biltcliffe, again and his Marxist Capitalist **3D** approach – the great thing is that it delivers impressive results (see earlier in the book).

Simon's approach to pushing continuous learning and development starts with himself. Simon is undertaking what he calls a DIY MBA. He has committed to one half day a week to learning and exploring. That means one half day consciously taking time out and

---

> reading books and magazines, browsing websites, listening to podcasts, and proactively going out to meet other people and visiting and learning from other businesses.
>
> It's a great example of 'fishing in different ponds' and he is encouraging others in his business to do the same.

So, what does this mean for you? Well, there is an abundance of resources out there (much of it 'free'), your challenge is to create some time to access and absorb it to increase your learning and knowledge and develop your own DIY MBA.

Go on, you know it makes sense – get your diary out, create an appointment with yourself and start 'fishing'.

So, rather than *always* looking to the same businesses for ideas that you *always* do, *always* tapping into the same trade associations that you *always* tap into, *always* visiting the same websites that you *always* do, *always* listening to the same podcasts you *always* listen to, *always* attending the same conferences and trade shows you *always* do, *always* visiting the same network meetings you *always* go to, *always* reading the same books, newspapers, magazines and trade journals you *always* do, why not do something different and see how other people, businesses, industries, countries, even 'cultures' actually 'do stuff' to 'differentiate' themselves?

Go on, it's relatively easy to do, and you never know what you might 'discover'?

Don't know what to visit, read, or see? Ask others what they recommend. What 'ponds' do they fish in? However, don't simply ask people who are just like you. Find out from people who have less in common with you. For example, if you're 'old', ask someone younger; if you're male, ask someone female, if you're in 'sales', ask someone in 'finance', if you're a 'techy' ask an 'artist', if you live in England, ask someone in the US, or even France (hey, it's 'revolutionary' stuff this!). Our point is, don't just ask people like you – there's a fair chance that they're 'fishing in the same ponds' as you.

It's about, trying new things, and maybe getting out of your 'comfort zone', but it doesn't have to be too extreme (if you don't want it to be).

Here's a simple little tip we picked up from someone Andy worked with many years ago who was a real 'forward thinker' and an extremely successful entrepreneur. Every now and then when Andy travelled by train, he 'fished in a different pond' by making a conscious effort to buy a magazine related to a topic or a sector he knew absolutely nothing about to see what he could 'learn'. Sometimes, it worked and he saw things he wasn't aware of or hadn't considered, sometimes it didn't, but the 'pluses' certainly outweighed the 'minuses', apart from being spotted at Newcastle station reading Hairdressers Monthly by a client! Obviously, with iPads, smart phones, social media, it's so much easier to get "fishing".

3D Demonstrated: 20% Time

Google have 20% time ... whereby their engineers have to spend 20% of their time working on their non-core activity. They base this on the principle that people do great stuff and generate fabulous ideas when they are working on things they are passionate about. Gmail was a direct result of 20% time. Just think, if you only allocated 2% of time on 'innovation' then you'd be 10% as good as Google, and that can't be bad.

Creativity and innovation is not prescriptive. What works for Google, won't necessarily work for you, but it *might*. Your challenge is to do something; one idea often leads to another. Hopefully, reading this has ignited a spark. Just do what works for you, or *might* just work for you.

Creating the right climate is about role modeling and encouraging others to follow suit! What are you like as a role model? How much time out do you consciously take out to make innovation work for you and your business? What do you do to encourage others?

3D Demonstrated: 'Stand In Other People's Shoes'

An engineering business established a very simple process to promote a climate of innovation. They set up an initiative called 'Stand In Other People's Shoes' where individuals shadowed their colleagues in other departments for a half day to learn what they did and how they did it. They established a very simple debrief process where individuals fed back... 1 thing that surprised them.... 1 thing that impressed them.... 1 thing they'd question.... 1 thing they'd do differently. Simple stuff, but it really encouraged cross departmental understanding, communication, working and business improvements – that's innovatiON!

3D Demonstrated: Tell Us How

Getting staff to generate ideas for improvement is a key characteristic of 3D Businesses. The best ones have processes to do this and here's an example from an organisation not probably noted for its innovativeness – the Civil Service.

'Tell Us How' is a process from The Cabinet Office that invites Civil Servants to put forward ideas to improve performance.

What we particularly like is the 'focus' that the initiative creates. For example, when it was launched in October 2011, the emphasis was on identifying ways to make work easier, reducing bureaucracy and overcoming 'blockages' to making this happen.

Since then, it has focused on taking this one
step further. It is specifically focused on the ways
management can realise potential. They are asking
civil servants to put forward their suggestions on
the practical things that could help them do their job
better, with particular emphasis on things that enable
them to:

- Be innovative and creative – implementing new
  ideas and taking a positive approach to risk;
- Achieve results – focusing on impact and
  outcomes, not just process and ticking boxes; and
- Work together – working well with people at
  different grades, organisations and locations.

Remember, our definition of innovation is 'the successful
exploitation of ideas', and it needs processes to make
this happen, so -

- **What 'processes' does your business have to
  encourage your people to generate ideas for
  improvement?**
- **How can you create 'focus' to generate ideas on
  the areas that count in your business?**
- **What can you do to ensure that something
  happens with those ideas?**

Making It Happen

Hopefully if you've got this far, you recognise that a lot of this is about **doing** things. Implementation is all about 'making it happen' and doing something with the ideas generated.

3D Businesses know that winners take action, not notes. Time, effort and resources are put into making things happen and this is monitored and measured – it is certainly not left to chance. They allocate time to do this and support this by measuring the number of ideas generated, and crucially the impacts they are making on the business.

We can say all sorts about this, and get wonderful quotes from world leaders, but we think it's best if we leave you with the words of wisdom of Dick Dastardly...

"Don't just stand there...
DO Something!!!"

You know it makes sense.

So , that's the last #Characteristic, number #7 ... Take a minute to reflect before we move to our conclusions :

- **What are the blockages to innovation in your business?**
  (hint... it might be you)

- **What 'processes' do you need to establish to make it work for you?**

- **What are you going to DO?**

"There is a better way to do it. Find it!"

Thomas Edison

And Now The End Is Near...

Of course it isn't. This is just the beginning. Hopefully we've got you 'thinking in **3D**' – your challenge is to keep doing it, and, obviously, to get others to do that too.

We hope that we've helped you recognise that **3D** thinking is a 'way of doing things' in your business. It's not a 'set of rules', it's a philosophy, it's an attitude, it's one that has to be shared and owned at every level of your business to really drive performance.

Of course, it looks different in every business, and there are no simple 'lists' of things to do, or 'rules' to follow. Your challenge is to 'establish' what your Dramatic Difference actually is, and Demonstrate that Difference in everything you do... keep doing .... and keep doing better! It's about leadership, it's about culture, it's about processes, and it's about people.

So, to finish, here are 7 more questions to get you '**3D thinking**'
1. Have you 'Got That Vision Thing' and is it giving you and your people a real focus and drive?
2. What's your 'Dramatic Difference' and do your customers and prospects recognise that in everything you do?
3. Are your customers truly 'Delighted' and 'Devoted'? (How do you know?)
4. Are you proactively Maximising your Relationships with the Customers you want to?
5. Does your culture support and enhance your 'Dramatic Difference'?
6. Are you maximising information to help you maximise performance?
7. Does 'innovation' really drive your business?

And some 'bonus' questions...
- **How do you know?**
- **What do others think (in and out of your business)?**
- **How can you find out?**

And finally...
- **What are you going to DO?**

Please do pass this on to others (or buy them a copy from www.andyhanselman.com), re-visit and re-read the book in six months' time, answer the questions again, redefine your priorities and rework out what you need to do.

Don't forget to celebrate your successes as well – with your people, and if you're up for it, with us too! We'd love to hear your success stories. You can email us at andy@andyhanselman.com or go to the website and share your thoughts and ideas with other '**3D** thinkers'.

Equally, if you have a query, suggestion or idea, please get in touch too – we can all learn from each other.

Thanks again - good luck, and keep '**thinking in 3D**'!

Just When You Thought It Was Over!
50 3D Mini Steps...

1. Pick out one idea from here and take action NOW!
2. Ring up or talk to ONE customer and ask *'What are we like to do business with?'*
3. Spot somebody doing something well in your business and thank them.
4. Identify your 'best' customers (How do you define 'best'?)
5. Consider getting rid of your worst customers (as a minimum, reduce your reliance on them and don't pursue others like them!)
6. Find out what your team think you should 'Stop, Start and Continue' doing as a leader.
7. Visit a website from another business or industry and see what you can learn.
8. Ask your suppliers and advisors *'How can you 'add value' to my business?'*
9. Stay at home to 'think and work' ON your business.
10. Read one of the books in our 'recommended reading' list at the end of this.
11. Generate five ideas to 'delight' your customers (Better still, get your team to do it), and then make it happen.
12. Ask others *'what's the first thing you would do here if you were the boss?'*
13. 'Stand in your own queues' - 'Get back to the floor', sit on reception, help out with deliveries, go out 'on the road'.
14. Google your company name, see what comes up.
15. Spend an hour consciously looking for your 'organisational stupidities'.
16. Get a team of your people to do the same.

17. What's the worst thing a competitor could do - how would you react?
18. Find one thing you always do that someone else could do.
19. If word of mouth really is the way forward (and it is), what's so amazing about you that makes people tell others?
20. Establish *precisely* how you are 'dramatically different'.
21. Generate ideas to work out how you can 'demonstrate' it!
22. Visit another business and see what you can learn.
23. Send one (some / all?) of your team out to do the same.
24. List the improvements you've made in the last 12 months.
25. Ask your people *'what information do you need to help you maximise performance?'* Consider giving it to them.
26. Consider putting (some of) your prices up
27. Identify one thing that you'd like to get better at in the next three months.
28. Ask your people *"What's the one thing we should never stop or change here?"*
29. Get your people to 'swap jobs' or 'shadow' each other - what can they learn from each other?
30. Ask your 3 key customers *'Why do you buy from us?'*
31. Share your 'wild ideas' with your people and / or some customers - what do they think?
32. Ring up your own business (and ask for yourself).
33. Get your people to describe your culture in just 3 words – 'post its' work well.
34. Set up a system that asks for referrals.

35. Give a team an amount of money and time to fix a specific problem in your business (let them identify it).
36. Take your office based people out to see customers.
37. Find an article on an issue affecting your business, copy it to your people, ask for their opinions and thoughts (maybe something from this book?).
38. Ask your customers *'who can we learn from?'*
39. Twenty minutes into your next team meeting, stop and ask *'how can we make this the best use of our time?'*
40. Find out if 10 of your customers really know about your full range of products and services.
41. Set and share a profit target - explore all the ways of achieving it.
42. Create a list of 'dream customers' and set a plan.
43. Let someone else chair your next team meeting.
44. Find out what your newest employee really thinks.
45. Visit a conference, exhibition or seminar, that's not directly related to your business.
46. Fast forward 12 months - what will you have in place?
47. Identify an award you can try and win, and go for it!
48. Spend an hour or two on your 'front line' – get on reception, answer phones, make a delivery, help in accounts.
49. Ask your people *'what one thing should I do better?*
50. Do none of these things, but **DO SOMETHING!** (and tell us what it is – we'll start a new list)

More Resources To Help You Get (And Keep) 'Thinking in 3D'!

Our Website...

We have put together a resource website that supports all the things discussed in this book (and more).

On it, you will find lots more information on the **3D** Demonstrated examples – there are videos, articles and links to websites. You'll also see more of our stuff – articles, toolkits, assessment tools and more examples of 3D Thinking.

You'll be able to 'sign up' for Andy's **3D** Thoughts – our short 3 minute podcast with 3iDeas every week, and to our monthly **3D** Digest e-newsletter – again, news, updates and links to things that get you **3D** thinking!

Books And Podcasts....

We love reading books, visiting websites and listening to podcasts – they can be a great source of **3D** iDeas, and people often ask us which ones we recommend.

Here's a short list we have put together we think are worth reading or listening to...

The ones we've put forward we think you'll find interesting, thought-provoking, or useful (and hopefully all three). It's only our opinion, so no guarantees here.

Please let us know if there are any others that you recommend – don't forget, we can all learn from each other.

Some Books Worth Reading...

Purple Cow – Seth Godin
Anything by Seth Godin is usually well worth a read, but if we had to choose just one, this would be it!

Loyalty Rules! – Frederick Reicheld
The book that explores the whys and wherefores of Net Promoter Score from the guy who created it.

The Richer Way – Julian Richer
Simple, but effective, customer service and people management stuff from one of the UK's best retailers (and employers)

The E Myth – Michael Gerber
Fantastic book on building a business by working ON it, not IN it – this is the one that got us started 20 years ago.

Delivering Happiness – Tony Hsieh
The story of Zappos by the guy who created it – an excellent story with really tangible lessons and examples – a must read!

Upside Down Management: A Common Sense Guide To Better Business – John Timpson
It does exactly what it says on the cover – some good, no nonsense ideas.

Rework: Change The Way You Work – Jason Fried and David Heinemeier Hansson
A stimulating and thought provoking approach from the guys who have created a truly **3D** business: 37 Signals.

Steve Jobs – Walter Isaacson

The story of one of the most famous **3D** thinkers – it's a fantastic insight into the (strange) mind of Steve Jobs.

A Book About Innocent : Our Story And Some Things We've Learned – Innocent

The title describes it! Great examples from the founders of Innocent Smoothies.

It's Not How Good You Are, It's How Good You Want To Be – Paul Arden

A short, irreverent, quirky guide to making the most of yourself.

Some Podcasts Worth Listening To...

Six Pixels Of Separation – Marketing And Communications Insights – Mitch Joel
A regular weekly update (every Sunday) from Mitch Joel at Twist Image – interviews and discussions with forward thinkers in the world of marketing and social media. Mitch is a really forward thinking bloke and always well worth a listen.

Duct Tape Marketing – John Jantsch
Marketing and business development tips from John Jantsch and his guests. John is an expert in helping growing businesses and many of his ideas translate very well cross the Atlantic.

Andy's 3D Thoughts – Guess Who?
Andy's short weekly podcast with 3 3D iDeas, rants, raves and examples in around 3 minutes every Monday morning. Short and sweet, just like him!

The Bottom Line With Evan Davis
BBC Radio 4's weekly business programme with discussions and debates on business topics chaired by Evan Davis.

Listen To Lucy – Lucy Kellaway
A weekly 'rant' from Financial Times columnist, Lucy Kellaway. It's a short sharp comment on a business topic – always tongue in cheek, often insightful, and always a good five minute listen.

Entrepreneurial Thought Leaders – Stanford Technology Venture Programme

A lecture to Stanford University students broadcast live each week during term time. You'll hear from incredibly successful entrepreneurs, academics, thought leaders and business thinkers sharing their stories, insights and learning. (The June 2013 one with Charity: Water's Scott Harrison is outstanding).

Office Hours – Daniel H. Pink

A monthly interview with a real business thinker by author Dan Pink – there are some real 'top people' in there, including Tom Peters, Biz Stone, and Jim Collins.

TED Radio Hour – NPR

A run through some of the ideas put forward via TED Talks that take place around the world. This one gets you thinking and often helps you 'fish in different ponds' by introducing things you'd never thought about (or even know about!).

Seth Godin's Start Up School – Seth Godin

This is brilliant! It's actually a live master-class with Seth Godin broken down into digestible 'chunks'. Insightful, practical and challenging – definitely worth a listen to the whole thing.

Desert Island Discs Archive – BBC

This epic series is an absolute 'institution' and you can listen to any and every guest who has appeared in it over the past 50 years – that's nearly 3,000 people! Of course, it's not all business related, but there's nothing wrong with that. Go through the archive and select who you want to hear from – but beware, it's a bit addictive.

Thank You's...

Putting a book together takes lots of time and effort, and help from lots of other people. These include....

- **All our clients who we have worked with, and built lots of friendships with over the last 20 years**

- **All the people who have shared our journey working for, and with us, over those 20 years**

- **Anyone who has ever been on one of our programmes, seminars or events**

- **Special thanks to Lucy and Danielle in our team who put up with us and have worked really hard on helping get this book out!**

And finally....

Thank YOU for reading it!